GOSPEL
BEAUTI*full*

MADDISEN SPANO

GOSPEL
BEAUTI*full*

BREAKING FREE FROM CHAOTIC FAITH TO
FIND WHOLENESS AND BEAUTY IN CHRIST

What people are saying about...

GOSPEL BEAUTI*full*

"Gospel Beautifull is such a breath of fresh air! There's knowing ABOUT Jesus and there's KNOWING Jesus. This book exposes all of those misconceptions and hurts we all have from religion and instead focuses our eyes on Jesus. Such an important read. Thank you, Maddisen, for saying not only what so many of us feel but also showing us how to heal and thrive—an intimate relationship with Jesus Christ." - Alison K.

"This book has completely transformed my view on religion & there's so much encouragement to cultivate a relationship with Jesus by the author while simultaneously, remembering that taking care of myself as a mom and wife isn't a bad thing! The author makes me feel like I'm sitting in a cafe with my best friend and makes you feel so loved!"- Adriah R.

"Gospel Beautifull was such an uplifting and beautifully written book. Encouraged me as a woman, mom, and believer in Christ. Highly recommend this book to women everywhere! Such a good read." - Gabby W.

"Gospel Beautifull radiates a profound sense of grace and enlightenment, captivating readers with its transformative narratives and spiritual depth!" - Andrea R.

"Gospel Beautifull" speaks to that little inner girl inside all of us who yearns for understanding, acceptance, and unconditional love. Maddisen speaks truth to the importance of relationship, and reminds readers that Gods love trumps worldly religion. He sees our beauty, He knows our heart. The journey to finding His love and our own identity through Christ is achievable no matter what our story may look like." - Bianca S.

"5 stars for Gospel Beautifull by Maddisen Spano. I so resonated with the authors experience with church and her faith as a child. Sharing how legalism and religion distorts our view of God. Bringing us closer to a real relationship with God and sharing how we can have freedom in Christ and develop a faith that is deeply rooted and authentic. Also, my favorite part of the book is the action pages with "tea time" just like your sitting with Mady with a cup of tea talking about Jesus. I really enjoyed the pink lettering and beautiful pages and look of this book! Just a joy to read!!" - Amie S.

"Not only did this book give me a new light on how I can unapologetically view and follow my faith but it gave me a new love for Christ and how I can easily get closer to Him. Reading a book where I'm able to relate and laugh?! I'll take it! More than anything Gospel Beautifull was a breath of fresh air, I've wanted to be closer to Christ without all the judgment and assignments…Maddisen showed me just that!!"
- Vyanka R.

"If you're churched out, tired, and hungry for Jesus alone this book is a God send. Maddisen's transparency and ability to cut straight to the heart made me feel seen in the same way I would chatting with a lifelong bestie over coffee."
- Kali S.

Gospel Beautifull

Cover photography by Alison Kissel Photography, LLC

This publication is designed to provide accurate and authoritative information in regard to the subject matter covered. It is sold with the understanding that neither the author nor the publisher is engaged in rendering legal, counseling, or other professional services. This book is intended for informational and inspirational purposes only. It is not a replacement for professional therapy, counseling, or medical advice. The author is not a licensed therapist or counselor, and the content within this book should not be considered a substitute for seeking appropriate professional help when needed. The author and publisher are not liable for any actions, decisions, or consequences resulting from the use of the information provided in this book. Readers are encouraged to consult with qualified professionals for any mental health or therapeutic concerns they may have.

All Scripture quotations, unless otherwise indicated, are taken from the Holy Bible, New International Version®, NIV®. Copyright ©1973, 1978, 1984, 2011 by Biblica, Inc.™ Used by permission of Zondervan. All rights reserved worldwide. www.zondervan.comThe "NIV" and "New International Version" are trademarks registered in the United States Patent and Trademark Office by Biblica, Inc.™Scripture quotations marked (ESV) are taken from the ESV® Bible (The Holy Bible, English Standard Version®), copyright © 2001 by Crossway, a publishing ministry of Good News Publishers. Used by permission. All rights reserved. Scripture quotations marked MSG are taken from The Message, copyright © 1993, 2002, 2018 by Eugene H. Peterson. Used by permission of NavPress. All rights reserved. Represented by Tyndale House Publishers. Scripture taken from the Amplified Bible, Copyright © 2015 by The Lockman Foundation. Used by permission. Scripture taken from the NEW AMERICAN STANDARD BIBLE, Copyright © 1960, 1962, 1963 1968, 1971, 1972, 1973 1975, 1977, 1995 by The Lockman Foundation All rights reserved Used by permission. http://www.Lockman.org

Printed in the United States of America
1st edition 2023

DEDICATED TO MY HUSBAND,
THANK YOU FOR BEING THE LIGHT IN MY LIFE, FOR YOUR UNWAVE-
RING LOVE, FOR ALWAYS CHEERING ME ON, AND FOR BEING THAT
SAFE PLACE I CAN ALWAYS COME BACK HOME TO, FROM WHICH I
CAN BOTH GROW AND CHASE MY DREAMS. I LOVE YOU.

AND TO MY SON, SILAS REMI. I LOVE YOU, MR. POO. YOU'VE GIVEN
ME THE COURAGE TO FACE MY STORMS SO THAT I CAN BE A BET-
TER MOMMA ALWAYS FOR YOU. YOU ARE MY SUNSHINE.

Contents

INTRODUCTION.

Hey girlfriend!

Oh my gosh, I'm SO thrilled you're here, flipping through the pages of this book with me! My heart is bursting with joy because what I really want for you is to find a happiness so true it feels almost like those Christmas Eve tingles—curious, delighted, waiting to unwrap all of life's gifts. This isn't just about Sunday morning, hymn-singing joy. I'm talking about rediscovering the spark you had as a kiddo and letting it light up your life. Why keep it all buttoned up and 'good-girl' serious? What's the point if we're not really connecting with God?

Now, let me keep it real for a second. I've got a small fear: What if my thoughts or experiences turn you off? Girl, please remember, I'm not perfect. I write from my own life experiences. But at the end of the day, I'm a work-in-progress just like you. What you're about to read are MY truths, my life lessons—take them as inspo, not gospel! I'm here to share my heart, not to preach at you. Life's about progress, not perfection, right?

My goal? To empower you to find YOUR kind of happiness and wholeness in Christ. Your own beautiful, unique path founded on the Lord, even if it's totally different from mine. Let's ditch the idea that faith has to be a one-size-fits-all experience, okay? Faith is a journey tailored just for you, ready to meet you in your own unique fears, struggles, and hopes. Like your favorite pair of jeans, our walk with Christ isn't one-size-fits-all. We each get a personalized, tailor-made journey. So, lean in, lean on Christ, and let Him be your foundation and guide through every high, low, and in-between. This book shares my own ups and downs and all the ways I'm striving for a richer, more connected life. I'm hoping you can connect with my own experiences and find encouragement as you work through your own. This book is here for you, especially if you're in a place where faith feels confusing, elusive, or just plain hard.

This book is like my diary, except I'm handing you the key. It's all about my fumbles, my 'ah-ha' moments, and my search for a life that's filled with what matters most. Plus, it's for every girl who's ever felt lost or confused and craves a faith that fits like her favorite pair of jeans.

Picture us right now, sitting in a café on a crisp Sunday in October, my fave month ever! Windows wide open, we're bathing in the warm glow of twinkle lights and seasonal scents, just chatting about life and love and faith. We're sipping on pumpkin spice lattes (basic, but delish!), just soaking up that autumn air, sharing our hopes and dreams. Feel it? Taste it? This is what our book journey is—a heart-to-heart convo between friends.

So, if you ever find yourself wondering, "How do I find happiness and wholeness as a Christian woman, even when life throws you curveballs, and religion sometimes makes you go 'hmm'?" Girl, this book is your gal pal saying, "Let's figure it out, together!"

Part 1:

WHEN YOU'RE CRAVING
A FAITH THAT FITS

1

THE CHURCH GIRL WHO DIDN'T QUITE FIT.

grew up in a home that didn't exactly do the whole church thing. So, when I found my way into the Southern Baptist community—the largest evangelical Protestant group—I was like a sponge, soaking it all in. I stepped into those grand, dark, wooden church doors at seven, eager for the messages about salvation and baptisms. But let me tell you, girl, the focus was on the "afterlife," not on making life "after" baptism any better!

THE EMPTY CUP

I was hurting, girl, from family stuff I didn't even know how to put into words. I wanted faith to fill that hole in my heart. But the more I prayed and sang hymns, the emptier I felt. It's like I was doing all these activities to rack up heavenly brownie points, but my own needs were still on the waiting list. The so-called "peace" I was chasing? It felt like a secret club that I wasn't invited to!

Don't get me wrong, saving souls is the Gospel call, but what about living the here and now? I was struggling emotionally because of my tough home life and needed some life-changing wisdom—stat!

But girl, I felt more weighed down by my faith than uplifted. It was like the church was saying, "Join our eternal VIP list, but don't expect any perks until you get there!"

TRYING SO HARD BUT FEELING SO EMPTY

I was that girl—the one who led Bible studies, volunteered everywhere, and basically lived in the church. I mean, I was ALL IN, okay? I was the poster child for being a devout Christian. I did all the church activities, mission trips, Bible studies, and even launched Christian groups at my school. But, my heart? It felt like an empty cup. I was so busy proving my faith that I had no time to enjoy it!

But inside? I was a mess. A hot, anxious, depressed mess. All my good deeds felt like empty calories—sweet but not filling. I wanted that joy, that peace, that 'Jesus glow,' but all I got was a reality check.

ARE YOU REALLY SAVED, THOUGH?

"Oh, honey, but are you sure you're saved?" my pastor would ask. I was saved enough for a stadium full of people at the Super Bowl on a Sunday. I had said the salvation prayer basically before breakfast and dinner, daily. Because for me it never seemed to deliver me from my fears of losing my salvation in Christ or it having just not "took" the time before. Perhaps I was "that one" that God had just not quite "predestined" for His Kingdom. Like Pastor had preached time and time before. But I kept praying and re-praying for salvation, like double-checking if I locked my car. What if it didn't "take" the first time, or the second, or the hundredth?

Trust me, if Salvation had a frequent flyer program, I'd have platinum status. I said those salvation prayers more often than I counted calories. But I was still wracked with fears, insecurities, and a gnawing emptiness. No peace, no joy, just a whole lot of 'What am I doing wrong?' feelings.

At a heart level, if I'm honest, I was empty and constantly hoped there was more to this faith which I was selling to everyone, including myself. I think I thought that if I just did what Pastor said, spread the good news, kept my purity intact, served where I was needed, and was a nice and good girl, the feelings would follow. They never did. Pastor was wrong about that. Things never did just 'sort themselves out'. I was severely depressed, anxious, and wildly insecure. My heart was full of so much fear all the time, and I never could quite feel that I measured up. I was either too much, or not enough. All the time. I lived this way for ten years. Selling this Gospel that had never even really reached me pre-eternity.

If I was saved, I certainly couldn't feel it. I felt just as lost as the world, except they all seemed to be having so much fun. And I wondered at times, why I was so unhappy if I was doing everything right- everything Pastor said. Surely, I've proven myself enough to start receiving what this Christian life promised. Right? Maybe not happiness, but joy at least- whatever that means. At this point, my faith felt so fake, so unreal, that I honestly felt like a fraud. Like a sleazy car salesman, I felt like I was selling a "lemon" to the world.

This was my life- if you can call it that- as a Christian for nearly a decade. Damage control, I guess. Not fully living, but not dying either- at least I had that. Until I felt that I'd rather die than live this way anymore.

BYE-BYE, CHURCHY LIFE

At some point, I realized, this is NOT what healthy love, even divine love, should feel like. Like stepping away from a toxic relationship, I took a break from organized religion. I started focusing on me, on what makes my soul happy. And, guess what happened? My life began to bloom!

I got to the point where I'd rather eat dirt than continue that way. So, I packed my bags, spiritually speaking, and took a break from the whole churchy thing. And girl, can I tell you? It was like taking off tight jeans at the end of the day. Ahhh.

For the first time, I felt like I was breathing. I re-discovered my passions and even started dreaming again. Religion had felt like an overcritical partner, always pointing out what I lacked. **But stepping away, I found a God who was all about love, not judgment—a God who wanted to heal me and make me whole.** Away from the noise and the "you-should-do-this" sermons, I found the God I'd been looking for all along. A God who didn't want me to check boxes but to live fully. And for the first time, I felt whole, like I'd been piecing together a puzzle, and I finally found the missing piece.

THE GOSPEL IS MORE

Over this journey of ridding myself of the only connection to God I'd known- God found me. But on His terms. And He taught me a gospel more than anything I've ever known. I found a God who was married to this material world which He had created and called "oh so good". I found God wasn't angry, oppressive, or hurtful at all, but that God loved me and healed the parts of me that were so fragile that I felt like I was being held together by a single unraveling thread. I found that God had finally done the work that ten years in the church could never do: He made me whole. Not separate from myself, my talents, passions, and dreams, but in them. What I've found through my lifetime spent in the religion of the evangelical church and what I want to share with you, dear reader, is this: I have been taught an incomplete gospel. The common day evangelical church is built upon half of the gospel where we get saved to go out and "do" but we miss the gospel that is for us, in us. The Holy Spirit came to save us, to come live in us, and change us. Not just for the sake of others, but for you and me. Personally. The Gospel I've come to see outside the church building is built upon a "happy God" who wants us to be happy too.

When we come to really know Him, we will start seeing the great divide between religion which claims a monopoly on Jesus versus a relationship which actually is the only way to Jesus. There is more that Jesus came to give us, and it's not found in the common day church experience which has become quite religious in nature. About doing, and busying, and traditions, and works. These things only clutter an already cluttered heart desperate for Jesus' rest.

I asked myself a few years back, why did I even come to the church? It was because I was in so much pain, and lived in so much fear. I needed a release from those things. Like me, most people come to religion because something is missing from our lives and we know we need more. Something outside of ourselves, beyond this world that is seen and felt. We want to know what's anchoring the beauty of our present world- the Maker with the keys to this fantastic now. We are searching for meaning and answers that no human can answer or fill. Ultimately our heart knows it is found in God. The Bible says the Creator of this world has written His truth on our conscience. We know He exists. He says he has written the evidence of Himself upon the world around.

And so we, those who have listened and leaned in, make the obvious connection to the missing piece in our lives: God. Our hearts serve to give confidence that this is what we were missing all along. However, the problem is that most find God in the common day spiritual experience which is often chalked up to church- the building. Just church. The problem with church is that we go to imperfect man to feed us God when we were meant to be fed by Him alone. Nobody else is worthy or true. Church can be wonderful, but it can also be flawed, because let's be real, it's run by humans! Instead of relying solely on a pastor or a congregation, what if you tried leaning into a relationship with God, directly?

Sweet friends, what I'm sharing with you is something I wish someone had whispered in my ear years ago: God isn't about do's and don'ts, He's about love and grace. It's not about a Sunday service checklist; it's about a personal relationship that enriches your every-day life. And, you don't have to fit into a cookie-cutter church mold to experience that.

Through this book, I want to tell what I have learned the hard way, the long way. The gospel is more. God came to bring happiness and all the things we are in want of at the deeper parts of ourselves. They matter! You matter! We go to religion to find our more but religion is actually the thing that harms us in our parts and keeps us from that more that He knew we needed and that He, through Christ, came to give. The solution is correcting the way we relate with God. It's breaking down our trust in tradition and the familiar to find an individualistic and intimate relationship with Christ where we are led by God and not by man.

Like leaving an abusive relationship we've got to leave the religious institution. If we are to gain our Gospel fullness in Christ then we must learn to think for ourselves, ask questions, and raise doubts. We need to learn to own our faith outside the church and be confident in the mess ups and getting it wrong. Because wrong we will get it at times, this Jesus thing, that is. But we are in fact covered by grace.

I'm encouraging you, as I wish I could go back all those years and encourage myself: We must learn to own our faith as individuals. We've got to stop placing our faith into the hands of the "experts", cuz they aren't experts at all.

The problem I find is that we go to religion to find God and religion is so far from God. Satan uses religion to harm our truest self. Doing further damage had we never come to the altar at all. Let's leave the altar call, and place ourselves at the feet of Jesus just like Mary did, without the Martha works. You may find, like Mary did, that Jesus was well pleased in her simple posture of stillness and expectancy. You may find, like Mary, a Jesus who fills like nothing the world or religion can do when we simply bring our hearts before Him simple-like.

YOU DO YOU, BOO!

Listen up, lovely ladies. A lot of us run to religion looking for something more—peace, love, you name it. But too often, we end up feeling like we're chasing our tails. What I've learned? We don't need a middleman between us and God. And we definitely don't need someone else's roadmap for our personal spiritual journey. Trust your intuition, ask the tough questions, and accept that you might mess up. Hey, that's what grace is for!

Own your faith journey like you own your style—unique to you and always evolving. Start questioning, start doubting, and please, for the love of all things holy, start owning your faith. Because no one gets to be the CEO of your spiritual life but Jesus. And guess what? It's okay to mess up. That's how you learn, how you grow, and how you come to realize that you're covered in grace, from head to toe.

So here's my nugget of wisdom: Ditch the altar call and make room for some real talk with Jesus. You might just find what you've been searching for all along. Stay tuned, sisters, 'cause we're just scratching the surface!

In the following chapters, I'll unpack how to bridge the gap between religion and a fulfilling, vibrant faith life. So, if you're feeling like you're stuck at a spiritual dead-end, take heart, beautiful. There's so much more awaiting you. The journey might be bumpy at times, but I promise you, the destination is absolutely worth it.

As a side note I will add that the first half of this book was written for those who have been hurt and damaged by harsh religion. If you don't vibe with this and this hasn't been your experience, then perhaps this book can serve as an understanding for those who have been. Or perhaps you are a new Christian. This can also be used as a tool to prevent such experiences. At the end of the day, no matter who you are or what your experiences with religion, this book can and should be used to break away from the common faith experience that's marginalized by religion. This book is for you. So feel free to skip to Part Three or even to Chapter 10 if you aren't vibing with my experiences that I share in the first half of the book. Once we get to Chapter Ten, we start hashing out a fresh and new way to own your faith. What that looks like scripturally. And how that looks personally.

Sending you all the love and light. Let's rediscover the fullness of faith together, shall we?

LET'S SPILL THE TEA, SIS!

Hey girl, it's time to sip some spiritual tea and dive deep!

> **Soul Resonance:** This chapter, girl. Did it speak to the depths of your soul? Did it feel like it was describing your own spiritual journey, complete with all its bumps and detours?

> **Heartfelt Check-in:** Honestly, do you ever feel like you're just going down a checklist with your spirituality? Like you're doing all the "right" things but your heart just isn't in it? If that's you, what's keeping you from finding that deeper connection?

> **The Emptiness Within:** It's hard, but let's be open here. Even with all the religious activities you're engaged in, do you ever lie in bed at night feeling like something crucial is missing? How does that emptiness make you feel?

> **Walking Away:** This is a tough one, but have you ever felt so disconnected or even hurt by a faith community that you had to step back? What led you to that breaking point? It's okay; your experience is valid.

> **Direct Line to God:** How personal is your relationship with God? Is it a one-on-one, heart-to-heart kind of deal, or do you feel like there's always someone or something standing in between you and Him?

> **A Loving, Gracious God:** The chapter talks about a God who is, above all, loving and full of grace. Does this image of God feel new to you? How does it affect you emotionally to think about God in this way?

Let's really connect on this, no holding back. Your heart, your experience, your spirituality—they're all valid, and they all matter. So, let's open up and share, shall we? Let's lay it all out, sis—no filters, no judgment, just pure, unadulterated soul chat.

2

THE LITTLE (G) 'GOD' OF RELIGION:

Let's Talk Real, Girlfriend!

Y ou know, looking back on my life, I totally get King
Solomon. No, I'm not claiming to be super wise or anything.
What resonates with me is his quest for more. Solomon, even
though he was super religious, couldn't shake this feeling of
emptiness. Sound familiar? The entire book of Ecclesiastes
is dedicated to his experiment with chasing that something more.
Solomon was a man who felt a deep pang of emptiness and
purposelessness. Whether it was some form of unknown at the
time depression, or identity crisis, or just the human experience of
longing- he went after this more. Just like all of us. He went in all
kinds of directions looking for meaning, happiness, and the purpose
of life. I find that He and I are kinda kindred spirits in this way.

THE SEARCH FOR SOMETHING MORE

Like Solomon, and like myself, each of us is on our own

#LifeJourney to find that elusive "more." And sometimes on our quest we end up putting our faith in all the wrong places. I'm talking about that "little (g) god" we find in some religious institutions. Sadly, this faux god is all about taking—our devotion, our hard-earned cash, and even our broken hearts—but what do we get back? Just a big ol' plate of guilt, shame, and emptiness. I've been there and it's like being stuck in a bad relationship with a god who just won't love you back.

LIFE BEFORE THE LITTLE (G) GOD

Growing up, my life wasn't a piece of cake. My mom did her absolute best, but let's face it, life was chaotic. With an absent step-dad and a full-time working mom, I had to step up and wear a lot of hats, but none of them said "just a girl" or "just me." It felt good being needed and depended on. I had a role, a purpose. Until it didn't feel so good anymore. I started asking, "What about me? What about what I need?" **Do I matter aside from what I could be doing for everybody else?**

BEING THE "GOOD GIRL" OF RELIGION

Ever find yourself in the role of the "Good Girl" when it comes to faith and spirituality? Trust me, I've been there. I wasn't raised in a church or spiritual setting, but somehow I became the self-taught poster girl for religious devotion. It felt like my upbringing had prepared me perfectly for it. Growing up my single mom depended on me so much that I found my sense of purpose in filling the only role that got me noticed.

Can you relate at all? Many of us find purpose in being the helper, the server, the doer. But let me tell you, even us "good girls" have our limits. There came a point where I was burnt out, emotionally drained, and anxiety-ridden. That's when it hit me: my sense of self-worth was entirely tied to how well I could serve others. My mom, my family, my friends, my God. I really didn't think I mattered outside of what I could do for someone or how I could be of benefit to them. I had no connection point to others outside of service. And it's lonely let me tell you. To think that your only worth and value is what you can do for others. It was a breath of fresh air to come to this realization that I matter just as I am. No conditions attached. After an entire lifetime of finding my value in what I can do for others. I want you to hear this: Jesus loves you. You matter to Him, just as you are, no conditions attached.

WHEN RELIGION BECOMES THE NEW TOXIC RELATION-SHIP

Isn't it just wild how our childhood beliefs and experiences can stick with us like stubborn glitter? You try to shake it off, but there it is, sparkling in all the wrong ways. I used to think my value was all about what I could do for others because that is what my value seemed to hold as a child. But hey, let's spill some truth tea: I've learned that I shouldn't have to earn the love, attention and acceptance of the people who claim to love me. I've learned that I can't earn God's love either and so it's pointless to try! This one-time "Queen of Earning Love by Doing It All" has definitely had her wake-up call. So, if you're walking a similar path, take this to heart: You don't need to work for Jesus's love—it's already yours, my dear. And really, anyone who says they love you should adore you simply for being you!

A GOD WHO GETS YOU AND LOVES YOU!

I've been on a figurative spiritual roller coaster: Methodist, Baptist, a sprinkle of Catholicism, and now? Just a gal who's head-over-heels for Jesus. And, let me tell ya, it's been a game-changer. We've all been told some version of God, right? But so many of us have got it, um, kinda wrong. Seriously, it's like we've been dating the wrong guy and missing out on Mr. Right! This whole mix-up has stolen our joy, yanked away our sense of purpose, and left us, well, kinda empty. And the tragedy? We've been missing out on the real, the original, the absolutely AMAZING Jesus.

Here's the tea, sis: Our wonky ideas about God have been messing with our minds, bodies, souls—our whole selves. Religion's been holding us back, like a bad hair day, but for our souls. Our misplaced understanding of God and the religion that we confine him to is messing with our heads and hearts. Religion is damaging us- emotionally, spiritually, and even physically.

I've hopped from church to church, met all kinds of pastors and even priests. And you know what's so heartbreaking? They're all haunted by this image of a 'little g' god who's more about guilt-trips than love. It's like they're stuck in a toxic relationship and they don't even know it!

So, moral of the story? God is not some abstract idea or guilt-tripping parent. He's this incredible, living, breathing love that we all so desperately need! Let's not get stuck in fear-based beliefs that just don't serve us, okay?

TRADITION VS. TRUTH

Now, don't get me wrong, traditions can be cozy and comforting, but they can also keep us stuck in a loop. If we want to grow, we've got to shake things up. And so, sis, as we wrap up this chapter, I have to get real with you. The way religion has been treating us? It's not just throwing us off our spiritual peace and wellness; it's impacting every part of who we are. Emotionally, mentally, physically, spiritually—it's all taking a hit. Imagine something that should be a source of life and joy actually doing the opposite, making us feel unloved and unworthy. Can you relate?

So, you might be wondering, 'Why is religion leaving us feeling more broken than whole?' This was my question too. It's like Satan has turned faith into this weird game of never feeling 'good enough.' Ever since he slithered his way into messing up Eve's relationship with God, he's been at it. That same divisive trick he played on Eve? It's been repackaged as modern-day religion, and let me tell you, it can do some serious emotional damage.

I want you to know there's more for you. You don't have to stay in a space that makes you feel less than the beautiful soul that God so lovingly created. I urge you—yes, URGE you—to look past the traditions and rituals that have bogged us down. Trust me, just because it's 'the way we've always done things' doesn't make it right or healthy. Iykyk. Breaking free from these bonds starts with questioning what we've been taught to accept. I know it's daunting. But if we want to live fulfilling lives as women who truly know Christ, then a big shift needs to happen.

Just like King Solomon was on a quest for 'more,' you have your own unique journey ahead of you. Let this book be a little nudge, helping you rediscover places within yourself you've forgotten or ignored. Who knows? It could serve as a roadmap to the you that God so beautifully designed.

Let's embark on this journey together, finding our authentic selves and the peace, happiness, and belonging that Christ intended for us all along.

THE REAL DEAL: FINDING YOUR MORE

This is my rallying call to you: Let's find transformation in a true understanding of God that exists beyond the constraints of religion! Let's embrace a Scriptural vision of God that's unclouded by our past experiences and ingrained beliefs. You've heard the saying, "knowledge is power," right? Well, the absence of knowledge can be downright reckless. Hosea 4:6 warns, "My people are destroyed for lack of knowledge." Too often, we entrust our spirituality, our understanding of ourselves, and even our view of God to mentors, tradition, or religious figures without really considering whether they genuinely know God—know Him in Spirit and in Truth.

We, the so-called 'good girls' of religion, sometimes unwittingly swap out the authentic Gospel for a diluted version that lacks the beautiful, redemptive qualities of Jesus. Why? Because we're conditioned to listen to our elders and avoid rocking the boat. Even when it grates against our spirit, even when it leaves us feeling less than whole, we push through and continue to uphold beliefs and traditions that others insist are 'correct.'

Without giving ourselves the room to think critically and discern the truth for ourselves, we run the risk that Hosea warned about: being "destroyed for lack of knowledge." We forfeit control of our own lives to others, often to our detriment.

So here's what I envision for us: a journey, a pilgrimage of sorts, similar to Solomon and other great figures of our faith. I want us to reclaim what we've lost or given away. I'm talking about a personal transformation—one that ushers us into a life bursting with genuine feelings, deep meaning, and unconditional love. A life where it's not religion but Jesus Himself guiding us, where our hearts and our true selves are cradled in the loving arms of a God who longs to be silenced by religion no more.

LET'S SPILL THE TEA, SIS!

Grab your fave mug because it's time for some soul-baring tea-time!

> **The "Solomon Complex":** You know how Solomon was out there searching for 'more,' only to find that life's real gems are far simpler? Let's get real—have you ever been on that quest, thinking that if you just had this or that, you'd finally be fulfilled? What was your journey like? And did you find what you were looking for?

> **Misplaced Faith:** Y'all, we've all been there, putting our faith in the wrong things or people. Whether it was that guy, a job, or even the 'perfect' IG life, where have you looked for fulfillment that ended up being a total dead-end?

> **Childhood Echoes:** Growing up, we learned a ton of stuff, but not all of it was good for our hearts and minds. Do you still hear those old-school beliefs or family expectations playing on loop in your head? How's that affecting your vibe today, especially when it comes to emotional and mental wellness?

> **#ApprovalGoals:** Let's talk about those 'standards' or 'goals' we feel like we have to reach to be loved or spiritually connected. Have you ever felt the weight of wanting to be perfect just so you'd feel worthy? What did that chase do to your soul health and overall wellbeing?

This is where we take off the filters and get into the nitty-gritty of our hearts and souls. It's all love here, so let's lean into the vulnerability, shall we?

3

AUTHENTICITY

Five years ago, my life felt far from what I had envisioned. I was grappling with emotions that were so overwhelming, I couldn't help but wonder, "Is this what feeling lost really feels like?" I was yearning for some sort of relief, a way to escape the emotional weight that felt like it was smothering me. And get this—on the surface, my life looked like a picture-perfect snapshot. I was newly married to my soulmate, and we'd just moved into our adorable first home. We were supposed to be living our happily ever after, floating in that blissful newlywed haze. We were at the starting line of the life we had both dreamt of and prayed for. So why did happiness feel so out of reach? Looking back on that difficult and confusing year, I can honestly say it felt like I was stuck in a maze that I couldn't figure out. And trust me, I'm not being dramatic.

CONFUSING PLACES

Let me tell you, I went back and forth so many times about whether or not to spill the tea on this part of my journey. At one point, I was like, "Nah, let's not go there," because my dream for this book was to help you all break free from the religious stigmas that trap us into thinking we can't live joyfully and wholeheartedly. I wanted to show you how to find that wholeness in Christ, outside the box of organized religion, just like I did. So, sharing this part of my story? I felt like it wasn't needed. I told myself that this book wasn't supposed to be all about me, but if I'm honest, what I really meant was that I didn't want you to see how far down the rabbit hole I'd gone. I wanted to present the Instagram-perfect Maddisen—the one who's got it all together—even if that wasn't always the real me. But then it hit me: I'd be skipping over the most crucial step in my healing journey—authenticity.

See, healing only comes when we get real—with ourselves, with God, and with the people around us. It starts when we're brave enough to share our less-than-perfect chapters, to be upfront about where we are, and to lay bare all the mixed-up emotions that come with it. And when we're met with open arms and love, that's when the light starts to seep in and the darkness loses its stronghold. So here I am, taking that leap and sharing this chapter of my life with you. Why? Because you're worth my authenticity, lovely reader. I hope it gives you the courage to shine some light into your own dark corners and find those grace-filled souls who'll listen to your story with nothing but compassion and empathy.

FACING THE DARKNESS

You know, my stepfather and I were never really close. He couldn't accept my twin brother and me as part of the package deal when he married my mom when we were just 2 years old. It felt like a constant reminder that we didn't quite fit in as his kids, or even fit in our own home. Every birthday turned into this miserable ordeal, and he had this countdown to our 18th birthday, like he couldn't wait for us to leave his house. In my teenage years, things got even crazier when he was arrested for domestic assault with a deadly weapon, and he threatened my family's safety. That left my mom as a single mom, and our family was hanging by a thread, nearly homeless. Can you even imagine how stressful that was for a young girl trying to figure out her way through the typical teenage chaos? And to top it off, throughout that next year, my stepfather decided to add to the pressure by sending me, personally, these threatening emails.

But you know what? There was a glimmer of hope. That's when my grandfather stepped in, offering me a safe place to live far away from all the chaos. Leaving my mom was hard and I felt like I was abandoning her, but I realized I couldn't carry her world on my shoulders anymore. Living with my grandpa, it was like finally getting to take a deep breath after holding it in for so long. He supported me in every way possible, and I felt loved in a way I'd never experienced before. Honestly, he spoiled me rotten. It all seemed like a divine intervention, a lifeline thrown to me by God. I believed that God was providing a way out and showing His hand in my life. I thought that the darkest days were behind me.

Then things took a dark turn. Over a few months, the sexual abuse started creeping in subtly, and I didn't even realize what was happening until I found myself stuck in a full-on nightmare. Depression and panic attacks became my constant companions. It's insane, but I started blaming myself because my grandpa, this respected figure, couldn't possibly be doing something so wrong, right? It took a friend's question to make me stop and think.

Eventually, we had to file police reports, but I still had to live in the same house as my abuser. It shattered my faith and made me question every belief I held dear.

I kept all of this buried deep down for years, but about five years ago I reached a breaking point. I couldn't keep pushing it away. I had to face my past and start the healing process. It was a time of deep introspection and questioning everything I thought I knew. It's just impossible to wrap your head around someone you loved so deeply doing something so terrible to you. A sort of death happens in your soul. It's a loss that feels all consuming. I loved my grandfather, and I still carry this pain with me today. It's something that's become a part of me, something I'll carry forever.

INVITING GOD INTO THE RAW AND THE REAL

And so yea, five years ago, I hit some sort of wall. I'd tried every-thing, and achieved everything that I thought would make me whole. I'd all but tapped out that religion thing, been the good girl, and after a lifetime of realizing that people pleasing and keeping in line never got me very far, I went to the opposite extreme. I went a little wild and let loose, partied throughout college, joined a sorority, and made some pretty stellar bad decisions. I really did relate to King Solomon in Ecclesiastes, I was experimenting with life. I was just trying to find happiness and a kind of wholeness that I'd never felt but always longed for. Skimming past college, I had gotten back on track with my life and religion and achieved my two major life goals. I'd gotten married to a great Christian guy and had a healthy baby boy- before the age of 25. I even bought my very own brand-new car. I had traveled a little and moved a lot. My five-year plan was on a fast track to success. As simple as my goals may seem- I had accomplished every 'big thing' I'd ever wanted to. Coming from the place I had come from these were pretty 'big things', indeed. But I wasn't happy. Quite the opposite.

I was miserable, depressed, in emotional anguish... every. single. day. I felt so guilty for so long and also a little confused. I should be happy, I would tell myself. So why am I more miserable than ever? Nothing particular happened when I got married except that I was finally free from the toxic life I'd always known. From my chaotic, emotionally unsafe childhood, from my abuser, from the fear I always felt growing up revolving around everything and everyone. And so let's ask the obvious together... What was my deal?

I guess to put my therapist's words simply, what happened when I got married is that I was finally safe. For the first time in my life, I could breathe without sh$# hitting the fan- pardon my French. I didn't have to fix my mother's problems anymore or deal with my abusive alcoholic stepfather. No more was I living in an unsafe environment, looking over my shoulder and locking my door at night. And guess what? My body didn't know what to do with it.

I wasn't a kid anymore tied to her parents' decisions and toxic behaviors. I was an adult, I was married, and I was my own person for the first time in my life. I was feeling the generational effects of my parents' sins. Heck, I'd lived in their consequences my entire life, helping them worm their way out of them. For once I was on my own, with only myself to worry about. It was just me, myself, and I. And my husband of course.

But what happened when I got married was that I took a turn down a dark alley. Quite inevitably. And there seemed to be no way of finding my way out of the maze of emotions. It was as if all the feelings and fear from my entire lifetime caught up with me and my body was no longer in fight or flight. No longer could I distract myself from my pain, or numb it. God placed me safely with my husband in a season of stillness and quiet where I had no distractions or noise. For once I could not silence the gnawing growls of the grave dis-ease which was growing within. It's almost like God knew something that I didn't, I had to feel it to heal it. And girl did I feel it. But instead of allowing my feelings to be indicators of areas I needed to heal, my feelings took full reign. I resigned to them and so I became a slave to them.

Pretty soon, alcohol and pills became my closest friend. I began cutting pretty badly. No, despite popular belief the self-harm I did was not for attention. For me, everything inside felt so dark and painful. It was as if I needed an outlet for all the pain I felt within, or else I'd explode. I'd go to church, lead my ninth-grade girls with a fake pink glossed smile plastered on my face, and two hours later be sitting in the shower with blood streaming from my self-inflicted wounds. My poor husband really went through the wringer those first few years. I thought I wanted to die.

At that moment in time, even through the counseling, I wasn't sure why I felt the way I did. I wasn't sure what I believed in. I didn't know who I was. It seemed to me that I was this little inky blob that just dropped onto a page. I was a mess and desperate to try and make something out of it all. The confusion and lack of understanding only made me feel like more of a mess up, which added to the emotional turmoil. What should have been the most exciting few years of my life became quite the opposite. Those three years became the longest, darkest years of my life. These years though became my hidden struggles. I locked up my true self from the world and let no one into the pain that was raging on the inside.

I assumed all my religious duties seemingly "fine"- like a nice Christian girl would. I went to church services, served, asked for surface-level prayer and prayed for others. But I had learned a long time ago that they don't do "messy" there. Just a little mess is fine, but the manageable kind. And for that, we'll pray for you! But no real to-life forms of help really come- no real lifelines are ever thrown out when we find ourselves in a sea of messiness. Certainly not for the full-on bat S#@t crazy kind of mess that I was feeling on the inside. Nope, keep that to yourself girl. So to myself, I kept.

But in myself, I was drowning. And after a few years of sinking deeper and deeper without a hope of getting out, I decided to try something new. I let go of my good-girl act with God which came, strings-attached, with religion. Really this was inevitable at some point. It was just too much work. It was exhausting. I didn't have the strength anymore to care about cleaning myself up before Him. The service and the guilt and the rules were some other things in the mix that I simply didn't care about anymore. I didn't have the mental capacity to fear or worry about whether or not I pleased God.

For the first time in my life, I just didn't care about being a good girl. Instead, I began to get raw and real with Him. The nice- ties of my religion were lost. Behind the scenes, I began stripping away all the 'spiritual' baggage- which for my whole life had kept me from really healing from my past or being happy in the present. And guess what? I was shocked that God didn't, in fact, strike me dead.

Yeah, going through hell did that to me. I lost all those amens and 'mea culpa's and 'forgive me Father, for I have sinned'- again. I just learned to get down and dirty, let the snot drip and the tears flow. No more pretty... God, this is me. Take it or leave it. And by the grace and goodness of God, He took it. He grabbed a hold of me during those three years where I wanted so badly to end my life and said uh uh girl, I got you. Let go. I'm here to take over when you don't have the strength. I did. And forgive my lack of good words, but whoa.

As I learned to lean into God without all that ridiculously stressful religious fluff, He showed up. He became everything I had ever needed. He became my healer, my counselor, and my alongside friend- when I didn't have the strength or courage to show up with anybody else. I had lost my religion and my fears of being unloved, and the rejection, and the trauma of abuse, and I done said, 'Lord, I'm never going back'! And in this place I was met with a God I had never known. A good God. Loving. Healing. Comforting. And happy. I'd met this amazing sweet caring Father who just wrapped me up and held on tight. Over a four-year period He had set me free from my oppressive anxiety and the heavy weight of depression. My mental disorders lost their grip altogether and I was freed to live beautifully. Today, I am weightless from all the things which used to hold me down like a thousand-pound sumo wrestler.

But this didn't happen overnight. There was no miraculous healing, at least not the instantaneous one which is often associated with large church gatherings and revival kind of things where we are "just healed" in the name of Jesus. Well, in the name of Jesus I was healed, but on Jesus' time table, not my own. Because sometimes instant healing isn't the point, it's the undoing that needs to be done. Undoing all the doings that got us where we are in the first place. All the lies we've believed, and the root problems, and the family trau-mas, and even the sin that we've gotten too comfortable with.

Honestly, Christian's get so focused on the spiritual revival sort of experiences, the modern-day miracles on YouTube channels and large-scale mega-church social feeds. That they miss the real work that needs to be done under the surface- the authentic, ugly, and uncomfortable healing. Not in your face, all for the show, we don't need to know all the details- be healed today but not tomorrow- kind of charade accompanied with lots of lights and musical productions, and cameras, and action. This isn't the kind of healing that came.

It came in the quiet, in the stillness, and through much help from counselors, self-reflection, forgiveness, and a few self-help books, yeah. But mostly it came because I had fought hard in prayer, in private, daily, morning by morning. Without fail. Jesus, who saw my authentic heart, met me there because it pleased Him to get away with me and do the dirty, hard work right alongside me. It pleased Jesus for me to get alone and get real with Him.

I wanted healing and I asked for it- like Jesus encourages us to do throughout the Gospels. He says, "ask and you shall receive". And so I asked, and I just didn't stop there. I went after it. I didn't just pray and then go sit on the sidelines fake smiling. Continuing on with my religious duties like nothing was wrong. Waiting for a miracle and then wondering why nothing was happening.

No, like a physical sickness, I felt the sickness of my soul and I took it to the healer, God. Like taking a hiatus from the church routine due to cancer, I put a stop to everything. I saw the growing disease within my soul which came with symptoms of depression, anxiety, and much unhappiness. And I felt the urgent need to do "church" differently and to withdraw from everything for a season so that God could do His therapeutic work without all the hustle-bustle and busyness that had always distracted me from the down and dirty work which Jesus was desperate to do with me.

I was at a place where I felt God calling me away from the "go out and tell the world" part of the gospel which had been the only gospel I'd ever known. Instead, He was inviting me to a gospel which receives Jesus as well. "Come to me all you weary and burdened and I will give you rest for your souls". He was urging me to come to the gardener so that He could do the restorative work within my soul. "I am the true vine, and my Father is the vinedresser. Every branch in me that does not bear fruit he takes away, and every branch that does bear fruit he prunes, so that it may bear more fruit." John 15:1-4 ESV.

Before I could go out and "do" once more, I needed to be healed-. And I mean roots deep, healed. I needed Jesus to cut off all the branches within that were broken, rotting, and hurting. The unforgiveness. The trauma. The lies I've believed. The sinful attitudes of my heart that I didn't even know were imprisoning me. There was a lot of gunk in my soul and what I needed was some spiritual surgery. And this wasn't going to happen in church. In the busy. In the noise. Nope, this was a work only Jesus could do. And for that He needed stillness. For the first time Jesus was calling me away from the gospel of "doing" and He was instead calling me to a gospel of "stillness" before His feet. So that He could cut off the branches that weren't bearing fruit so that for once, I could bear clean fruit for the Lord. All in time.

LET'S GET REAL, LOVES: UNPACKING A BIG CHURCH MYTH

There's a common misconception in church circles. "Just give your life to Jesus, and all your worries, mistakes, and pains will magically vanish." Let's be honest, we'd all love for it to be that simple. Look, I'm the first to stand up and testify that miracles do happen. I've seen and felt things that can only be described as divine. And yet, I think it's time we have a heart-to-heart about this. Because, for the vast majority of us—I'm talking 99.99%—our walk with Christ is just that: a walk, a journey. It's not an 'overnight' Amazon delivery service; and we don't just magically 'arrive', cutie friend. When you open your heart to Jesus, you're starting an incredible journey that's going to have its fair share of bumps, detours, and moments where you want to pull over and take a break. And guess what? That's perfectly okay. That's how we grow, how we dig deep into what our souls are yearning for. This process takes a lot of courage, some soul-searching, and a fair bit of vulnerability.

But, lovelies, you're never alone in this. The encouragement, prayers, and compassion from your spiritual family can be your lifeline. They're not just people you see on Sunday; they're your sisters and brothers in this wild, beautiful ride of faith. They're the ones you can turn to when the journey feels a little too heavy to handle on your own.

So, as much as I adore the incredible, life-altering moments of divine intervention, let's be honest and gentle with ourselves. Faith is a process. It's a series of steps—some easy, some challenging—but each one is an important part of your journey to becoming more whole and connected to Christ, yourself, and others. And what's beautiful is that we're all in this together, step by step, lifting each other up, and drawing closer to something much greater than ourselves.

AUTHENTIC CHURCH

Listen, friend, I've got to level with you, heart to heart. Living in this era of #authenticity is a genuine blessing—no air quotes needed. We're peeling back layers, getting real about mental health, and finally learning to embrace our flaws and all. But let me tell you, the church still needs a serious reality check.

Picture this: an ad campaign for Christianity that looks like it was shot for Vogue. Everyone's hair is perfect, smiles are sparkling—the whole thing is just too pretty to touch. But is that what we truly yearn for? Heck no. What we want is something real. We want to know we're not alone when we're feeling like we're at rock bottom. We want to feel seen, cellulite and all. We need spaces where we can talk about our messes and know that someone will be there to help us clean up, not judge us for the spill.

Here's the tea: it's time for the church to unbutton that top button, loosen that tie, and get down to earth with us. Those leaders on their pedestals? Time's up. They need to take a seat—right here, next to us, in the trenches. They need to open up about their own struggles so we can all be free to be authentic, without shame.

And we need to stop pretending the church is this pristine palace of perfection. Because, honestly, that's not helping—it's hurting. It's isolating. And it's high time we say it: the church doesn't have all the answers, but that's totally fine. You know why? Because Jesus does.

In my life—I'm spilling the truth here—transformation didn't come like a lightning bolt from the sky. It came slowly, gently, in the arms of a community willing to see me—flaws, scars, and all—and say, "You're welcome here." It came from conversations that had more awkward pauses than scripted prayers, more raw tears than rehearsed testimonies. And that's exactly where the magic happens, right in the middle of our mess. **So let's lead the way and say, "Enough of this curated Christianity. Let's be real, let's invite Jesus into that mess, and let's transform together."** Because, sweet friend, that's where the genuine miracles happen.

REFUGEE IN NEED OF JESUS

Let me lay it on you straight. When I first walked into the church, I felt like a refugee, ya know? Like I was running from a world that had been so harsh and cruel to me. All I wanted—seriously, all I needed—was some warmth and comfort. I wanted to feel like I'd stepped into a hot shower or wrapped myself in a cozy blanket. I needed some soul food, both literally and spiritually. But instead, what did I get? A "Jesus Lite" experience, as if someone took all the good stuff out and left me with empty calories. They saw my mess, poked at it, and just called it "sin," as if that label could make it go away. They couldn't deal with it because, let's be real, religion can be so surface-level.

So listen to this: the church, as much as it promises to be a sanctuary for the lost and hurting, often falls so short. Instead of lifting us up, it judges and condemns the very people who are just trying to be real about their faith. Because come on, we've all got our struggles, our past, and our doubts. But the church wants us to shove all that under a rug, like some sort of "Don't ask, don't tell" policy for the soul. And that's not life. That's just putting on a performance in a religious drama where the script doesn't allow for any real human emotions.

What I've learned the hard way is that the church's

shallowness made me ashamed of my own brokenness. I never felt whole. I lived in these separate worlds: one for church, one for everyday life, and one for the deep-down pain I couldn't show to anyone. The message I got was, "Look pretty and put-together for the people we're trying to save." How messed up is that?

So I ended up bouncing between these separate worlds, never feeling like I belonged entirely to any of them. And it's not just me; it's a whole lot of people who feel they can't bring their full selves to church. They go looking for healing in other places because the church has made it clear that it doesn't have room for real-life problems. But then they get judged for seeking help elsewhere! It's like a no-win situation.

And don't even get me started on how the church avoids dealing with real, emotional pain. Remember those Bible stories where religious folks just walked past the guy who was beaten and left for dead? Yeah, that's still happening. We see each other's pain, but it's like we don't have the tools or the training to deal with it. And somewhere along the way, we lost sight of what's really important—love. I mean, the Jesus I fell in love with from the Bible was all about love. He felt things deeply. He cried. He was moved by people's pain and stepped in to help.

The truth is, you can't separate the spiritual from the emotional. And that's where I find the modern church falling short. The Jesus I know is nothing like the shallow, out-of-touch religious culture we see today. He was there for the broken, the downtrodden, the stigmatized—people like Mary Magdalene and the Samaritan woman. He didn't just promise them heaven; he gave them living water for their parched souls right here, right now.

So, what if we, as a church, could be more like that? What if we could be a place where people feel seen and heard in their pain? Where we can all be our authentic selves and find healing together? That's the dream, sis. And it starts with showing up—mess and all—and allowing others to do the same. That's how we can live out the Gospel in both spirit and truth. And I believe we can get there, one brave and honest step at a time.

LET'S SPILL THE TEA, SIS!

> **Picture-Perfect or Real Life?:** So, be honest—how much are you filtering your life, especially when you're around your squad, posting on Insta, or even just chatting with friends? What's stopping you from just being 100% you? Like, if you could get real for a sec, what's something you wish you could spill to someone without judgment?

> **#GoodGirl or #RealGirl?:** In terms of your spiritual walk, are you giving everyone this "I'm fine, it's all good" vibe, or are you opening up about your uncertainties and what's really bothering you? How raw are you willing to get with God? He can handle it, trust me.

> **Ghosting Your Feels or Healing Your Soul?:** We've all been there—sometimes it's easier to just ignore those nagging emotions, am I right? But what happens when you actually stop swiping and deep-dive into understanding and sorting out your emotional stuff? Are you holding space for your own healing?

This is the real talk that takes us from surface-level to soul-level so that we can really be 'whole' women who impact the world around us in authentic ways. Let's embrace the messy, the real, and the heartfelt as we sift through it all. It's all welcome here, boo!

Part 2 :

WHEN YOU'RE DONE
PLAYING BY THE RULES

4

THE DAMAGE WHICH RELIGION HAS DONE TO OUR SOUL :

A Split Self

You know, my husband Vincent is deep into his college classes, majoring in Psychology, and the more he learns, the more I'm struck by the profound parallels between psychological well-being and spiritual health. Picture a chair, sturdy and balanced, standing on four legs. Each leg is essential; take one away, and the whole thing topples over. In many ways, we are a lot like that chair—comprised of four distinct but interrelated parts: mind, body, soul, and spirit. For us to be fully upright, fully functioning, all four legs of our 'chair' have to be in sync, solid, and well-tended.

This leads me to something Vincent shared with me: dissociative identity disorder, also known as multiple personality disorder. This isn't an inborn condition. It emerges when a person, often a child, experiences severe neglect or abuse. To cope, the mind splinters itself, creating separate 'identities,' like a chair losing a leg and desperately trying to stay upright by any means necessary. It's a

defense mechanism, a tragic fragmentation of the soul that happens when the natural need for love and care is unmet.

So, where does religion fit into all of this? Well, I'm grappling with a haunting parallel. Religion, especially when it's rigid and punitive, can splinter our 'chair,' too. It can weaken one or more of those legs—mind, body, soul, spirit—until our whole being is compromised. Religion can make us neglect essential parts of ourselves, all under the guise of devotion or the quest for 'holiness.'

Satan has used religion as a guise to assault our inner makeup. He's been breaking our figurative chair down since the beginning of time! He's used the guise of religion to disassociate us from the parts of us which were meant to all function together as a whole. What has happened over centuries is this: religion has taught us to disassociate with our 'selves' as God intended us to be, if we are to attain holiness or reach God. We are starved for God's love as we are. This changes us. At every turn, we feel his sprawling anger and in turn deface our inner selves for all the ways we feel we aren't measuring up.

The collateral damage is real, especially for those who have been deeply immersed in religious environments. It's like we've been trained to prioritize one 'leg' while neglecting the others. Our spirit may be in hyper-focus, while our emotional well-being (our soul) is ignored or even suppressed. The result? An internal schism, a fracture in the unified 'self' that God intended us to be. So get this, I'm a visual person and I'm betting you are too. So to help you visualize this whole chair analogy I've created a visual-aid to help. It's a little wonky but the idea is as good as Gospel.

I can't stress how critical this is: to bring our 'chair' back into alignment, we must give voice to this unspoken division, this internal fracturing caused by dogmatic faith. This chapter, then, is an earnest attempt to delve into that—so that we can restore the balance, mend the broken legs, and finally achieve the wholeness we've been missing. This is the cornerstone concept that I'll be threading throughout this book, so let's not just skim the surface. We're going for deep repair and holistic understanding, okay sis? Because a chair with a wobbly leg isn't just a chair issue—it's a stability issue affecting everything that chair is meant to support.

As we closed the last chapter, we grappled with the painful reality of how religion has done a number on our souls. It's as if one of the legs on our chair is cracked, making it nearly impossible to feel secure or stable. Now, let's peel back the layers and get real about what religion has been telling us, so we can understand how to mend our chair and ourselves.

YOU'RE NOT CANCELLED: THE RELIGION TRAP AND FINDING YOUR AUTHENTIC SELF

Okay, so we're in an age of cancel culture, right? Well, religion has been trying to "cancel" people for centuries—cancel their dreams, their identities, and even their joy. Isn't it ironic that in a world so keen on individuality, religious dogma often demands the opposite?

You've probably seen the hashtags: #SelfCareSunday, #MentalHealthMatters, or #DoYou. Well, here's the real tea— religion frequently insists you're not enough as you are. It says, "Dial down your dreams, your gifts, and your emotions. Only then will you be holy."

Sound familiar? We're living in a world obsessed with hustle culture; yet religion tells you that your ambitions and goals are irrelevant unless they're confined to the chapel. That's like telling a plant it can only grow in a box with no sunlight or soil. It doesn't work like that.

And let's talk about the 'Minimalist Movement.' We've Marie Kondo-ed our homes and lives, keeping only what "sparks joy." But religion often teaches us to chuck out the very things that spark the most joy—our passions, our dreams, and even friendships outside our faith circles. They say it's all in the name of 'simplifying,' but it feels a lot like erasing to me.

Here's where we need a vibe check. Religion often acts like a toxic ex, making us walk on eggshells, thinking we'll never be enough. It's a gaslighting narrative that's more about control than communion with God. When we're in harmony with God, our soul becomes our higher or true self. Yet, if our soul is deprived of a deep, fulfilling relationship with God, it suffers. We become like a chair missing a leg—unstable and unable to stand firmly. Emotional and mental turmoil ensues because our soul craves its true purpose: to be with God. When religion rejects our true selves, the results can be devastating. Many end up leaving the community of faith, not realizing it was never Christ who rejected them.

So, as we carry on, let's remember that our chair—our whole self—deserves to be stable and complete. We've got to recognize how religion has distorted the truth so we can rebuild that chair leg and sit firmly in our relationship with God so that He can be the foundation beneath our figurative chair.

It's a heartbreaking truth that many people seeking Christ have been duped by this incomplete and distorted version of the gospel. Jesus didn't ask us to kill off the 'self' He created lovingly; He asked us to reject our 'sinful self,' which are two completely different things. Sin, when looked at correctly, is a form of self-harm, harm to others, and harm to our relationship with God.

But here's the kicker: This isn't about religion versus spirituality; this is about misconstrued religion versus authentic faith. Religion says, "Hide your true self," but authentic faith says, "Come as you are."

So, in a world where 'cancel culture' and 'hustle culture' pull us in opposite directions, remember this: God's love doesn't cancel anyone, and His grace doesn't require you to hustle. You were designed to flourish, not just exist.

And if you're worried that straying from traditional religious norms will make you lose your community, think about this: Even in the age of social distancing, we've found new, meaningful ways to connect. God's community is more inclusive and expansive than a single doctrine or building. So let's flip the script, shall we? **Aligning with our Creator isn't just about surviving; it's about thriving.** So go ahead, be unapologetically you. God's not cancelling you; He's celebrating the beauty that He created!

YOUR UNIQUE CONNECTION WITH GOD: WHAT RELIGION GETS WRONG

Alright, lovely reader, we've already chatted about the heavy stuff—how religion has been kind of a soul-crusher, am I right? But now, let's pivot and focus on the divine sparkle that religion often ignores: your one-of-a-kind relationship with Jesus.

So here's the deal. Religion loves to say, "Die to yourself," but hold up! They're twisting God's words. What God actually said is more like, "Let go of your sin-filled self." That's a whole different vibe, sis! Listen, this misconception isn't just a tiny oopsie—it's led so many of us down a path of spiritual hurt and confusion. God made you unique for a reason, babe, and it's not so you could squash yourself into some religious mold. Nope, He gave you all your quirks and passions to actually bring you closer to Him.

So when religion tries to stamp out your sparkle, remember: God wants you to shine for His glory not fade away. He's calling you to ditch the stuff that keeps you from Him, not the amazing traits that make you, well, you! Keep this in your heart, lovely: your personal journey with God is truly unique, and that's not just acceptable—it's a spiritual necessity. Our faith has to become our own.

INDIVIDUALISM IN CHRIST

I remember being 14 years old when I rededicated my life to the Lord. Though I've always been a driven and creative person, I felt like I had to give all that up. The message the modern-day church sent was clear: to serve Christ, you must sacrifice everything. Maybe I took that message too far, but it led me to believe I had to give up, well, just about everything. Growing up, the church never taught me that my unique talents, passions, and personality could bring me closer to God—let alone glorify Him. Instead, religion seemed to shame individualism, painting it as self-promoting. The narrative was all about serving, tithing, more serving, and sacrifice. Don't misunderstand; these acts are meaningful when they come from a place of freedom, not fear. But that freedom in Christ was something I never learned about. So I mistakenly believed I was earning God's love by sidelining my own dreams and passions, which caused me deep grief.

For years, I "died to myself," believing this was what God called me to do. When it came time to go to college, I chose the most religious institution I could think of: Moody Bible Institute. I celebrated my acceptance letter! But as I considered my options for a major—Christian ministry, Old Testament Survey, Biblical Languages, Jewish Studies, Missional Leadership—I realized I had no passion for these subjects. This filled me with dread. I wondered, "Am I less of a Christian for feeling this way?"

This is where modern religious experience falters. It teaches us that we must sacrifice all that makes us who we are if we truly want to love God. It sets our soul at odds with our God-given needs and wiring. Religion says happiness is reserved for heaven and demands we must "die to ourselves" here and now. But in God's Kingdom, you can indeed "have your cake and eat it too." You can find both eternal security and immediate happiness. There's no need to choose between them. God created us as we are, and when He is at the center of our lives, joy naturally follows.

It's as if religion is so fearful of God's holiness that it wants to keep us at arm's length, making many live lives devoid of enjoying God right where they are. It's a sad and ironic scenario. That's part of why I felt compelled to write this book. I want you to know you're not any less a Christian, or less loved by God, or less of a person because you don't aspire to a theology degree. This makes you unique. In God's eyes, you are precious exactly as you are. It would be tragic to betray how God made you just to comply with religious legalism.

Here's the freeing truth: God designed you with a dual purpose—1) to bring you closer to Him as you explore your talents, joys, and dreams, and 2) to reflect an aspect of Him in whatever you're called to do, be it through His creativity, beauty, or something else altogether. Contrary to what the religious elite might think, we aren't all called to reflect God in the same way. God is intricate and values our unique abilities to connect with and reflect Him in ways only we can. Just as a lion portrays the ferocious majesty of a God demanding respect, a flower reflects a God so intensely romantic that He longs to be adored. Everything in creation plays its unique role in reflecting and relating to God, and that's beautiful.

The hard truth is that religion often instructs us to suppress the very traits where the Spirit wants to flourish, to not only bring us joy but also glory to God. To live a life both glorifying to God and beneficial to ourselves and others, we need to embrace our God-given uniqueness. However, before we can do that, some repair work is essential. We must discard the legalistic religion that suffocates our true selves. How can you identify such religion? One telltale sign is always legalism.

LEGALISM ASSAULTS OUR TRUEST SELF!

You know how we've been talking about this whole chair analogy, right? That we're like a chair with four legs—body, soul, spirit, and mind? We need each of these legs to be sturdy if we're going to stand up and live the full life that Christ has intended for us.

But let's be real—how many of us have felt overwhelmingly guilty because legalism insists we must adhere to out-of-touch spiritual standards and expectations 24/7? It's as if taking a moment for self-care, scheduling a therapy session, or even considering medication for your mental health suddenly makes you 'too worldly' or 'not spiritual enough.' Raise your hand if you've ever been there. Enter legalism, the enforcer of strict rules in the religious world.

Just when you're starting to embrace life and prioritize taking care of yourself, legalism shows up with its restrictions. It's like that one person who insists you follow a rigid path, making you feel uncomfortable about seeking help for your mental health or simply needing some extra TLC. We're all about living authentically and embracing life in all its facets, including the good, the bad, and the ugly. It's crucial not to feel like we're stepping out of our relationship with God if we seek mental health support, face struggles, or simply need a little self-compassion.

Now, the Bible does talk about a spiritual life, but nowhere does it say we should neglect the other parts that make us whole and balanced. This is where legalism takes a wrong turn, adding extra rules and baggage that weigh down the joyous, fulfilling life we're meant to have in Christ. Remember, our faith is meant to be liberating, not confining. However, too often, I've heard preachers and pastors misuse verses, taking them wildly out of context to defend an unrealistic and out-of-touch spirituality that leaves no room for actually 'living' and embracing authenticity in this complex world where things aren't always so black and white. Scripture warns us about these pitfalls; it cautions that leaders, and even Satan, can twist God's words to lead us astray (Matthew 4:1-11; Ephesians 6:10-18; Galatians 5:1). I mean, just look at the Gospels when Satan literally used the Bible against Jesus! Can you imagine? Manipulating God with His very own Word? Our common enemy is pretty audacious. He does the same to us too, all the time! Scripture tells us that the enemy comes to 'steal, kill, and destroy' (John 10:10), and often, he accomplishes this through legalism, which ultimately harms us.

So let's not be deceived, friends. Legalism isn't just touching our spirituality; it's messing with our true selves, including our minds, bodies, and souls. But the good news is this: we don't have to let it. Christ came so that we could have life, and have it abundantly—not just in the sweet by-and-by, but right here, right now.

LET'S SPILL THE TEA:

> **Soul Check-In:** How's your faith playing into your daily life? Is your spiritual foundation strong, giving you balance — emotionally, physically, and mentally? Or is it a little broken and wobbly, affecting the other intrinsic parts of you? Do you ever feel like religion guilts you into focusing too much on one aspect (or figurative chair leg) and ignore the others? It's easy to get out of balance, am I right?

> **The "Perfect" Woman Mask:** Real talk, sis. Have you ever felt like you've got to play down your true self to fit this mold that you think your religious community wants? Whether it's the way you express your feelings, your ambitions, or even your personal style—have you ever felt pressured to hide parts of the fabulous you that God created and loves?

> **Seeking Approval or Seeking God?:** In your circle, do you feel like you're cherished for the individual that God lovingly crafted, or do you feel like you're in this never-ending race towards some "holiness" finish line that keeps moving further away?

> **Twisted Truths:** Have religious "do's and don'ts" ever made you or your girlfriends misunderstand what it actually takes to be close to God, or what true spiritual strength really is? How does that make you feel deep down?

> **Be You, Unapologetically:** Lastly, how are you striking that sweet balance between staying true to the unique person God created—the things you love, your talents, your emotions—and

allowing it to connect you with God? Have you ever thought that maybe you were created uniquely to reflect a little bit of our intricate God in a way only you can?

These convos can be heavy, but they're so needed. Let's keep it real and heartfelt as we navigate this faith journey together!

5

IT'S TIME TO BREAK UP WITH LEGALISM AND SAY 'HELLO' TO YOUR GOSPEL-GLOW UP!

et's go there, sis. Have you ever been stuck in a relationship that was just, well, bad news from the get-go? You know, the kind where your love life feels like a never-ending episode of a bad reality TV show? Yep, I've all been there. Now, what if I told you that's exactly how legalism in religion feels— like that toxic ex you keep going back to even when you know it's doing you zero favors. But today's the day we finally hit "unfollow" on that mess. So grab your favorite cozy blanket and your go-to comfort Stanley; we're diving into how to break up with legalism and embrace the full, fabulous life that the Gospel offers. You in? Cool, let's do this.

BREAKING UP WITH LEGALISM: WHY IT'S TIME TO STOP SETTLING FOR A TOXIC SPIRITUAL JOURNEY

Legalism is basically that bad-boyfriend stereotype who promises the moon and stars but delivers a whole lot of nothing. It's the spiritual equivalent of a "situationship" that leads to a dead-end. Sure, you started out thinking this was "The One"—you know, the belief system that would make you a better person, bring you closer to God, and perhaps even guarantee you a V.I.P ticket to heaven. But over time, you start to realize that things are not as rosy as they seemed. In fact, it's quite the opposite. This relationship, built on endless rules and guilt trips, is literally suffocating your soul.

Enough with that! Just like you shouldn't settle for less in your love life, don't settle for a second-rate spiritual journey either. It's time to break up with legalism, and girl, this one's gonna stick.

FROM COSMIC RED PEN TO GRACE: DITCHING THE ANXIETY OF A PERFORMANCE-BASED FAITH

You've been there too, right? Those sleepless nights where it feels like you're on a spiritual roller coaster that just won't stop. I mean, how messed up is it to be living in this constant fear of "Am I doing enough? Am I good enough for God?" We've been programmed to think our spiritual worth is somehow tied to a performance score-card. Cue the night sweats and 3 a.m. crisis prayers. Every. Single. Night. I would wake up, literally dripping in anxiety, hitting my knees to rattle off a laundry list of "sins" that I was pretty sure had landed me on God's naughty list.

Here's the crazy part: My faith felt like a job with impossible KPIs (Key Performance Indicators, for those non-corporate peeps). Even after doing my "best," I still felt like I was missing the mark, like God was up there with a cosmic red pen just waiting to mark me as a failure. Ugh!

Okay, so fast-forward to one Wednesday night after youth group. My girlfriends and I are perched on this brick wall outside church, doing the usual post-service chit chat and giggles. Only this time, I decide to get super real. I spill all about my relentless fears of losing my salvation, the crippling anxiety that came with it, and even my deep-rooted fears that maybe, just maybe, I was never predestined to be saved in the first place.

I braced myself for judgment, for that age-old sermon of "You just need to work out your salvation, girl. Do better." But guess what they said instead? "Me too." Yup. These girls, these strong, faith-filled women I looked up to, were wrestling with the exact same fears. Now, these were girls who've grown up in the church, who had Christian parents, girls who deeply loved the Lord. It was like someone had flicked on a light inside me. If they were grappling with this stuff, despite their strong faith backgrounds, then there was definitely something twisted happening in our church culture.

That's when it hit me: we've become a congregation of Christ-fearers, not Christ-lovers. And y'all, that's not the life God wants for us. We're gonna dig deep into breaking this cycle because I've got news for you: your Gospel glow-up is way overdue.

YOUR FAITH MAKEOVER: DITCHING LEGALISM FOR A LOVE STORY WITH GOD

Let's get one thing straight: God wants a love story with us, not a horror story where we're trembling in fear. So let's make that our mission in these pages—to reconnect with a God who's been tragically misunderstood by religion and legalism. We're kicking that toxic spiritual baggage to the curb. Because let's be honest, it's as if we've been sitting on a three-legged chair, and our spiritual leg is just splintered, thanks to all the religious hoops we thought we had to jump through. You ready for this? Grab your makeup remover and wash your face because, girl, we're getting a faith makeover. The goal here is wholeness, my friend—complete, unshackled you-ness, connected with the divine. So if you're bold enough to venture into this no-turning-back journey, you'll find a sense of completeness that no amount of Sunday school guilt-trips could ever give you. Stick with me through this book; your Gospel good news is coming, and trust me, it's way better than what we've been spoon-fed all this time. And to really lay down some truth, let's dig into the Good Book. Matthew 15:1-3 says, *"Then some Pharisees and scribes came to Jesus from Jerusalem saying, 'Why do your disciples transgress the tradition of the elders?' And He answered and said to them, 'Why do you yourselves transgress the commandment of God for the sake of your tradition?'"*

Ouch, right? Jesus isn't pulling any punches here. Then 2 Corinthians 3:6 comes in with the mic drop: "The letter kills, but the Spirit gives life." Boom! Say it louder for the people in the back! Now, let's get historical for a sec. Legalism? Yeah, that's not new; it's as old as the Pharisees. Despite the wrap that Pharisees got they actually started off pretty solid. They were like the spiritual life coaches of their time, trying to bring people back to God. But then they got all tangled up in rules, regulations, and 'you-better-do-this-or-else' vibes. Sadly, that kind of thinking is still wreaking havoc today, showing up in different denominations and even cult-like Christian groups.

As Pastor and Christian writer Joe McKeever puts it, "Legalism betrays Christ, violates the Gospel, and destroys people...

**The legalist is smarter than God... He insists his way is
the only one and can play the more-righteous-than-thou
card when we do not agree with him.**"[1] Yikes!

Let's not mince words: legalism is like that toxic ex who
keeps sliding into your DMs, messing with your spiritual wellbeing.
It's got its claws deep in many women, so much so that they can't
even imagine life without it. But here's the cold, hard truth: if fear
is making you clutch onto your religious rulebook, then you're in
spiritual quicksand. Because fear, sis, doesn't come from God; it's a
surefire sign that you're shackled.

So here's the tea: This book is your spiritual detox. We're
cleansing out all that religious clutter to make room for a more
joyful, more authentic relationship with God. Are you in? Because,
girlfriend, it's time for your Gospel glow-up, and it's gonna be
fabulous! If you're nodding along, let's get down to business. By
the time you reach the last page of this book, I want you to feel like
you've just cut loose a weighty anchor. I want you to say, "Yes, THIS
is what I want. I'm breaking up with worldly religion, and I'm all in
for the love affair God actually wants with me." But before we get
to that aha moment, let's name the enemy for what he is and say,
"Satan, not today!" With that said, take a look at this 'Is Legalism
Affecting My Faith?' quiz I created. Take a few minutes, or as much
time as you need, to really answer this quiz with your heart.

If you found yourself nodding "yes" to four or more
questions, it's time for some spiritual spring cleaning, sis. Let's dig
deep and sift through what you believe and why. Take it from me,
breaking up with religion can feel like stepping into uncharted
waters. But trust me, it's where you find your true North—God
Himself.

IS *legalism* AFFECTING MY FAITH?

CHECK ALL THAT APPLY.

Do you focus more on what you can do for God than what He's done for you? ☐

Does your church stress good deeds to win God's favor? ☐

Feel like God loves you more when you're "good"? ☐

Can't say no when asked to serve? ☐

Hold back on personal style to fit a religious image? ☐

Feel distant from God even after asking for forgiveness? ☐

Avoid people who have different beliefs or lifestyles? ☐

Struggle to share your personal issues with others? ☐

Always feeling judged by God and others? ☐

Uncomfortable when someone gives you a gift? Feel indebted? ☐

See life in black and white, with no gray areas? Or areas of "discussion"? ☐

Believe there is little to no room for opinion or disagreement in theology? ☐

Feel disconnected from God if you miss a Sunday service? ☐

Obsess over meeting your own high standards? Not just in faith, but life, too? ☐

IS *legalism* AFFECTING MY FAITH?

CHECK ALL THAT APPLY.

Hard to have close relationships with people, for fear of rejection? ☐

Quick to be "judgy" with yourself and others? ☐

Prayer and Bible-reading just items on your to-do list? But don't really get to your heart? ☐

Think God's blessings are rewards for "perfectly" falling in line? ☐

View the world as a dark place to avoid? Not to be en-joy-ed? ☐

Believe God is often disappointed with you? ☐

Quick to label differing opinions as "wrong" or even "sin"? ☐

Many conversion "experiences", but still doubt your salvation? ☐

Struggle to feel close to God unless you're "doing" something? ☐

Is legalism affecting my faith? ↓

Count how many boxes you checked. *2-3 - a smidge*
4-5 - moderately
6-8 - a pretty good amount
9 or more - I'm bound

WHEN LEGALISM HURTS OUR *Gospel* IDENTITY

LEGALISM BREEDS PRIDE

Ladies, legalism isn't just a pride-generator; it's a full-on pride nourisher. It can lead us away from trusting in God and towards relying on our own deeds, making us think we're the ones in control. But remember, the Gospel teaches us that salvation and our standing with God are gifts through Christ, not earned by our own works (Ephesians 2:8-9).

LEGALISM HOLDS YOU CAPTIVE

Legalism's constant scrutiny of motives, thoughts, and actions, whether in ourselves or others, blinds us to the simple freedom in Christ. Galatians 5:1 warns us: 'For freedom, Christ has set us free. Stand firm; don't be burdened again by the yoke of slavery.'

LEGALISM BREEDS FEAR: THE OPPOSITE OF GOD'S LOVE

Legalism breeds fear, diverting focus from God's love. Crafted by Satan, it traps believers in a cycle of dread, hindering them from experiencing God's freedom, blessings, and true standing after salvation. As 1 John 4:18 says, 'Perfect love drives out fear.'

LEGALISM BREEDS ISOLATION: THE TRAP OF SHAME AND BLAME

Legalism often assigns blame and isolates us, leading to shame and cutting off vital connections with God and supportive community. Satan exploits this, making us feel alone in our struggles and shame.

LEGALISM KILLS YOUR INNER CHILD

Legalism suggests that it's not the heart that counts before God, but rather our strict control and religious OCD. In adhering to this mindset, the legalist sacrifices her childlike joy and trust in Christ, her Savior. He died for her precisely so she wouldn't have to be perfect to stand confidently before God.

LEGALISM BLOCKS SPIRITUAL DISCERNMENT

Legalism manipulates the Bible to serve its own agenda, isolating verses from context and imposing interpretations through a 'law' lens. It overlooks the Holy Spirit's role in revealing deeper meanings of Scripture, surpassing human knowledge and experience.

LEGALISM CONFUSES 'FEELING' WITH CONSCIENCE

Legalism misinterprets shame and condemnation as God's judgment, elevating human emotions to divine communication without critically testing the spirits, which can manifest as implanted thoughts and feelings. Scripture advises discernment in 1 John 4:1-6.

LEGALISM CUTS OFF OUR LINK TO GOD

Legalism damages our faith and disconnects us from God. God bridged the gap between our flaws and His perfection through Jesus. His sacrifice set us free from the fractured faith seen in the Old Testament.

Ask yourself these questions. Is religion driving your relationship with God, like some sort of spiritual GPS that's actually leading you off course? Are you always on high alert, scouring your life for failures not based on God's standards, but your own? And be real—if you're a perfectionist or a people-pleaser, are you hustling for your worthiness?

Legalists think they're living under some divine magnifying glass, where God is just waiting to go, "Aha! Gotcha!" But, girl, that's not the God we see in the Bible. God isn't checking off a to-do list of your actions. He wants to know YOU, your heart, your dreams, your fears—no strings attached. Isn't it time to question how we've gotten God so wrong?

KICKING THE SPIRITUAL CHORE LIST TO THE CURB: EMBRACING A LOVE-FIRST FAITH

Look, the traditional church often turns the God experience into a spiritual chore list. They make it all about climbing some spiritual corporate ladder, which only kicks the chair out from under us. But listen up: Jesus shattered that myth. He showed us through the Pharisees that you can follow every rule in the book and still miss the whole point—Him. So here's the grand finale: We're saying goodbye to legalism and rediscovering the God who is all about love, not checklists. I promise, once you take that leap, you'll find a Jesus who's been waiting to catch you all along.

Alright, let's bring it all home. True religion? It's love, pure and simple. It's not about nitpicking your flaws or making you feel like you're never enough. That's just legalism in disguise, and let me tell you, it's a buzzkill for your soul. So whether you're holding onto your religious rulebook because that's how you were raised, or you're scared to rock the boat—listen up: none of that serves you. When Christ's love isn't the foundation of your faith, everything wobbles. It's like trying to sit on a chair with broken legs—sooner or later, you're going down.

DISCLAIMER ALERT

Don't get me wrong. I'm all about stirring the pot. I want you to side-eye the church you've been loyal to, rethink your denomination, and even question how you relate to your spiritual leaders. There's a revival bubbling up, and Jesus is separating the wheat from the chaff. He's showing us what the Gospel really is: pure, powerful, and deeply personal.

Take this with you as you close this chapter: the church is NOT a stand-in for Jesus. In fact, sometimes the church can actually muddy your understanding of the real, transformative Gospel. So be cautious about placing your whole heart in the hands of a human institution, because, girl, not even your fave pastor has all the answers.

From my own journey, I've seen that most Christians— including those at the pulpit—aren't living in the freedom Christ offers. They're stuck in this spiritual limbo, reciting salvation prayers but not really grasping what Jesus' freedom truly means. Don't let that be you! Your relationship with God should be your own, not some secondhand version passed down from others.

So, if you want to be a light in this world, you've got to own your faith. No more just going through the motions or borrowing someone else's beliefs. We're talking about embracing the Gospel in its fullness. Only then can you be the vibrant, effective witness this world so desperately needs. It's time to ditch empty religion and start living out a faith that's as real and authentic as you are. Are you with me? Because, honey, we've got some soul work to do!

LET'S SPILL THE TEA, SIS!

Life's already a lot, and faith shouldn't be another stressor, right? It should be our safe haven! So let's spill the tea:

> **Real Talk Time:** Girl, have you ever had one of those late-night convos with your besties or fam about what salvation really means? You know, the low-key fears, the doubts, all of it. What did they say, and did it resonate with you or just add more questions?

> **Rule Breaker or Heart Taker:** Do you ever feel like your relationship with God is less about love and more about a long list of dos and don'ts? What's that doing for your spiritual life?

> **#AdultingIsHard:** Okay, let's be real. Does your faith ever feel like another job, but with impossible "KPIs" (Key Performance Indicators) you can't ever meet? How's that messing with your everyday vibe? And how can we turn our faith into a connection point with God that is more of a place of rest, not yet another place to strive?

> **Fear Factor:** Are we just a squad of "Christ-fearers" at this point, living in fear of doing something wrong, instead of being "Christ-lovers" who embrace love and grace? Thoughts?

> **Culture Check:** What's the tea on church culture? Are there specific traditions or teachings that you think are fueling this whole "legalistic" mindset we talked about in the chapter?

This is a safe space, girl. Let's unpack it together.

6

THE FEAR FACTOR:

When Religion Stops Being a Safe Haven

ey girl, let's have some real talk. Have you ever felt like fear just followed you everywhere? If so, you're not alone. Let me take you down memory lane. I grew up haunted by fear. It hung over me like a dark cloud. I was scared of losing my mom to her depression, scared of not having enough, scared of my step-dad when he had one too many. Heck, I was even scared of the guy who was supposed to protect me- later on in my adolescent years. Fear was this invisible chain that just wouldn't let me be.

I looked to the church for solace, hoping it would be my sanctuary from the storm. But can I be honest? The church was anything but peaceful for me. I was living on pins and needles, worried that if I messed up just once, I'd lose God's love or even my salvation. Can you imagine that? As if it wasn't enough, my abuser wore the disguise of a godly man. I'm talking about a life-long deacon, a Bible study teacher, and a mentor. But his spiritual facade crumbled, revealing a man far from the God he claimed to serve. This twisted reality got me thinking. It's time we challenge the weight we give to our religious institutions and the people who lead them. We're talking about men and women who are part of the body of Christ, the church. How much should we really depend on them to connect us to a loving, holy God?

Stay with me, because we're about to unpack why religion often brews a toxic cocktail of fear, and how we can free ourselves to experience the authentic love and peace that Jesus brings.

RELIGION BREEDS FEAR, ANXIETY, AND UNDERMINES OUR STABILITY: THE MENTAL HEALTH CONNECTION

Let's get into the nitty-gritty about fear, anxiety, and depression, because these emotional culprits aren't just messing with our spiritual lives; they're wreaking havoc on our mental health too. So sit down, prop up your feet, and let's unpack how fear doesn't just shake our life's metaphorical chair—it's also the silent instigator behind a host of mental health issues.

You see, our bodies are beautifully complex, but they weren't designed to live in a continuous state of "fight or flight." So when our adrenal glands are working overtime, churning out adrenaline and cortisol, they're not just affecting our physical state. These hormones have a direct line to our brain, affecting our emotional and mental well-being. Studies have shown that high cortisol levels are often linked to symptoms of anxiety and depression. In fact, they mess with the balance of neurotransmitters in your brain—those crucial chemical messengers responsible for mood regulation. So you're not just "feeling off"; your brain chemistry is actually altered, which can lead to chronic anxiety and depressive disorders.

Additionally, this persistent fear and stress can contribute to other mental health issues like Obsessive-Compulsive Disorder (OCD), Post-Traumatic Stress Disorder (PTSD), and even Generalized Anxiety Disorder (GAD). And these conditions often become a vicious cycle, feeding off each other and making it incredibly hard to break free.

Here's something mind-blowing: The Bible gives us a daily prescription against fear. It literally tells us "Do not fear" 366 times. That's like a year-round mental health tip straight from the Divine, with a bonus for leap year! Yet, how paradoxical is it that many of us, seeking solace from these very fears, anxieties, and depressions, turn to religion? We yearn for something that assures us, only to find out that sometimes religion itself can fuel the fear and imbalance we're trying to escape.

So what's the takeaway? Let's stop letting fear, often accentuated by misplaced religious fervor, rob us of the balance and peace we're designed to experience.

SCARING THE HELL OUT OF ME

If you've ever felt your heart race as a street preacher declared, "You're all going to hell!" you're not alone. I was just seven when that message seared into my young mind. The fear was real, and it led me on a desperate search for God—not for love or understanding, but out of pure, gut-wrenching fear. Fear isn't just an emotion; it's a powerful motivator that often drives us straight into the arms of religion. But what if I told you that religion, for all its promises of salvation, often just amplifies that fear? You're scared of not being 'good enough,' of missing out on blessings, or even of eternal damnation. And religion? It eats that fear up like fuel for a never-ending fire.

Bertrand Russell was a philosopher who quite openly said he wasn't a Christian during a time when Christianity was the wide road taken. He argued that religion was all about fear: fear of the unknown, fear of defeat, even fear of death. Now, I may not agree with all of Russell's viewpoints, but he nailed it when it comes to the fear factor in religion.

However, there's a twist to this story. Russell's criticisms, ironically enough, echo the very teachings of the Bible he disregarded. The Bible tells us clearly: "There is no fear in love, but perfect love casts out fear" (1 John 4:18 NIV). Fear and love, according to the very faith that many claim to follow, cannot coexist.

The crazy part? Even Russell, an avowed atheist, agreed on this. He wrote that love banishes fear and that fear leads to cruelty. If you've felt religion's cruelty—the constant pressure to do more, be more, and never, ever mess up—then you know that Russell was onto something.[2]

So, does this mean we abandon all faith? Of course not, but it means we need to question what we're really chasing: God's love or our own fear-driven ideas of Him.

So, if you're hanging onto faith out of fear, it's time to reassess. Are you chasing after a love-filled relationship with God, or are you running scared, held hostage by a religion that thrives on your fear? It's a question worth pondering, and the answer could reshape your entire spiritual journey.

THE UNSPOKEN SUFFERING: WHEN FAITH BECOMES FEAR

Who hasn't had an "all or nothing" attitude at least once, especially when it comes to our spiritual journeys? We're after the whole enchilada: peace, joy, and that deep, unconditional love. But let's pull the curtain back—how many of us are actually caught in a cycle of paralyzing fear instead? If you're nodding your head, trust me, you're far from alone.

You've heard those sermons, haven't you? The ones that leave you in cold sweats, questioning whether you've done enough to be "saved." If you messed up, well, you must've said the salvation prayer all wrong. Isn't it ironic how these messages of "unconditional love" suddenly come with a ton of conditions? Welcome to the twisted maze of legalism.

DEBUNKING LEGALISM: THE UNMASKING OF A SPIRITUAL BUZZKILL

POINT I: LEGALISM SAYS "DO MORE," JESUS SAYS "YOU'RE ENOUGH, IN ME"

When Jesus spoke in Matthew 11:28, he obliterated the exhausting treadmill of religious striving. Feeling weary? Overwhelmed? Spiritually fried? Jesus says, "Come find peace with me." He's not demanding you prove your worth; instead, he welcomes you into a grace-filled relationship. Think about it—this is a faith that lets you fully embrace your humanity.

POINT 2: THE EGO TRAP: LEGALISM MAKES IT ABOUT US, NOT GOD

Let's get it straight—legalism is self-centered to the core. It puts the focus squarely on us, our actions, and how "good" we can be. It's the height of spiritual narcissism. Instead of looking to what Jesus did for us on the cross, it turns the spotlight on us. It's like we're trying to outshine Jesus Himself, and that's just not how it works, ya'll.

POINT 3: LEGALISM—THE KILLJOY OF LIFE AND FAITH

Legalism drains the life out of everything good, pleasurable, and humane about existence. It tells us that enjoying the simple pleasures of life is sinful, denying us a full, abundant life with God. Legalism is that annoying friend who shows up uninvited, overstays their welcome, and ruins the party for everyone.

THE MENTAL TOLL: LEGALISM'S ASSAULT ON WHOLENESS

Let's address the elephant in the room—this toxic cocktail of legalism and fear can wreak havoc on your mental health. You end up anxious, stressed, and far from the wholeness and happiness God desires for you. The simple joy and peace that should come from a relationship with God get swallowed up in an ocean of "shoulds" and "musts." It's exhausting and spiritually destructive.

THE HEART OF THE MATTER

At the end of the day, legalism and religion are like conjoined twins, each feeding off the other's toxicity. They circle you into an endless loop of inadequacy, snuffing out the beauty of a genuine relationship with God. It took me falling away from my faith to realize how much they had robbed me of my inner peace and happiness.

YOU'RE MORE THAN YOUR TO-DO LIST

If you're seeking solace and safety, let me tell you, religion and its twin, legalism, are not your sanctuaries. Far from it. They'll make your already heavy burdens even heavier, leaving you broken and far from the God who just wants to love you as you are, in Him.

So, don't let legalism and its fear tactics rob you of the beautiful, enriching, and yes, human, experience of faith. A faith that doesn't ask you to be perfect, but just to be you.

If you're like most people, you have your own fears and struggles that perhaps lead you to seek comfort in church. While God is undoubtedly there to offer solace, it's crucial to distinguish that from the pitfalls of organized religion and its inseparable twin, legalism. These two entities don't offer you a sanctuary; instead, they compound your existing burdens. They add to your list of "to-dos," fuel your guilt, and whisper ever so subtly that you are never enough- even through Christ. They continuously crucify Christ as if His death and resurrection- the first time- weren't more than sufficient to cover our sin. In doing so, they undermine the very wholeness and joy found in genuine spiritual communion. The gospel's straight-forward message—that you are loved unconditionally through Jesus Christ—gets lost in the mix. So, don't be deceived; your true spiritual refuge isn't in endless striving but in embracing the liberating love of a risen King. Hallelujah for that! Amen.

LET'S SPILL THE TEA, SIS!

Religion or Anxiety?: Have you ever turned to religion hoping to find some inner peace, only to feel like you ended up with a suitcase full of fears and anxieties instead? What's up with that?

> **Stress Check:** How often do you stop and think about how that non-stop stress and worry could be messing with your mental health? Self-care isn't just face masks and bubble baths, you know.

> **Mental Toll:** Have you felt like your mental well-being is taking hits because of some rigid, fear-based religious teachings? Let's unpack that a little.

> **God's Guidelines vs. Toxic Rules:** How do you tell the difference between having a healthy respect for God's guidelines and falling into that trap of toxic legalism that just makes you feel guilty all the time?

> **The Joy Snatchers:** In your spiritual journey, have you noticed moments where the "shoulds" and "musts" totally robbed you of the joy and peace you were originally looking for in God?

> **Seeking Wholeness:** What does "wholeness" mean to you, and does it vibe with where your faith is at right now? Are you finding that the 'whole you' fits into your spiritual life, or are there conflicts you're wrestling with?

I hope these questions get you diving deep into your faith and your feelings, encouraging you to find that balance that makes you feel whole. Your spiritual journey should uplift you, not bring you down. Despite what you may be used to, our faith is supposed to be a safe space where every part of us thrives and flourishes on the foundation of our good God! When we align ourselves with the ways of our good God, we reap the benefits of living the way that we were designed to all along- fully!

Part 3:

WHEN YOU'RE READY TO

Flourish

7

MY HAPPY PLACE

You know, I thought about naming this book 'Girl, Own Your Happy'. Maybe that's a title for a next book, but for this one, I felt I had to dig deep into all the religious jargon that can mislead us into thinking God doesn't allow us happiness. I figured a religious gal might recoil at the notion of Owning Your Happy. And let's be real, in the marketing world, it would be a cardinal sin to name my book something that seemed so outlandish to my intended audience. I'd be torpedoing my credibility as a Christian author before I even got started! I wrestled with the notion of even daring to discuss happiness in a Christian nonfiction work. You know as well as I do that 'happiness' is almost a taboo word in religious circles. It's lumped in the same category as 'sex,' 'feminism,' or 'self-love.' Those words just don't sit well in the prim and proper life of a religious gal. We're supposed to be above all that worldly and fleshly stuff, right?

But then I asked myself, "How can I not share what I've found?" How could I keep this treasure, this jewel of knowledge, to myself? This jewel has brought me a freedom and excitement in my faith that I never knew was possible. So, I couldn't, in good conscience, keep it locked away. I'm talking about a forbidden treasure in the evangelical realm—something almost unspoken. And that is this: God might actually want us to be happy. Not just that, but He could very well be the source of that happiness. Imagine that!

In many religious circles, the pursuit of happiness is subtly and yet powerfully discouraged. There's a kind of whispered fear that God might just strike our name out of the Book of Life if we dare to find joy in this material world. We've been taught that our goal should only be to evangelize, to spread the Word to everyone we know. And happiness? That's not a part of the equation. We've all heard it: "God desires your holiness, not your happiness." It's almost like an unsaid rule: Be holy, not happy. Got it?

But what if I told you that's not the whole story? What if I told you that I've found permission from God Himself to rebel against that teaching? Even more, what if God doesn't just permit happiness but actively invites us to experience it? Dear sister, I don't just have a permission slip to roam the halls of happiness; I have a personal invitation from the Bible itself to luxuriate in a realm of joy. As it turns out, we Christians—or 'Christ imitators'—are called to higher things than mere legalism and rules rooted in fear. We're called to live lives that are not just holy but also happy.

OUR HAPPY PLACE

God intended for our spiritual lives to anchor the happiness and wholeness that, let's face it, we're all seeking—either directly or indirectly. I've noticed that many of us church-girls are almost passive-aggressively scrapping for permission to be happy within our faith. We're desperate for a God who doesn't force us to choose between our spiritual selves and our deepest desires. A God who doesn't push us to fragment ourselves into disjointed parts, or worse, to negate our very existence.

Listen up, sister: True happiness kicks in when we, flaws and all, sync up heart-to-heart with our Creator. Imagine a connection so deep and so creatively personal, there's no box it can fit in. Forget rules. Forget limits. It's all about an intimate heart-to-heart, soul-to-soul dance with God Himself. It's the coziest, most comforting connection you could ever dream of.

This happens when we stop begging permission from the religious naysayers, and instead give ourselves the only permission we ever really needed: our own. Doing this allows us to tap into the magnificence that comes from living in communion with the Almighty and embracing our authentic, God-created selves. When we sense that God loves us for who we are, something magical takes place. Legalism gives way to passion. Fear is usurped by love. And stale religion blossoms into a living relationship.

This is what I like to call our soul's "happy place," where we're free to just be, and where all aspects of "us" are wholeheartedly welcomed and adored.

GOSPEL FULL

For centuries, the church has drummed it into our heads: God doesn't want us happy. He wants us joyful, they clarify, as if happiness is a step too far, a line not to be crossed. It's too worldly, they say. Too self-focused. Too emotional. Too real. But what if I told you that's not the whole gospel truth? What if I told you that God not only wants us to be happy but also intends to satisfy our deep craving for authentic meaning and purpose, reflecting His own divine happiness?

Life doesn't have to be a mosaic of disjointed moments of spiritual 'joy' that feels distant and out of touch. Happiness—defined through the raw, unfiltered lens of Scripture, untouched by the veils of tradition, legalism, and human interpretation—can be the cornerstone of a gospel-centered life. Listen up, dear sisters: You can live a gospel-driven life and be genuinely happy. A feeling of abundance, purpose, and wholeness can be the continual gift we receive from a gospel-oriented lifestyle. In essence, our happiness is our "Gospel Fullness." Our faith is rooted in a happy God who wants to flood our lives, fill our cups to the brim with His unbounded joy.

UNLOCKING GOSPEL JOY: THE 'GOOD NEWS' SHOULD RESONATE IN YOUR SOUL TODAY, NOT JUST IN THE AFTER-LIFE

Now, to experience this Gospel Fullness, we have to be willing to receive it, don't we? The issue is, many of us have only heard of a version of the gospel that's...well, not all that joyful outside of the promise of heavenly pearly gates. Isn't the gospel supposed to be preached now and experienced later? It becomes difficult to welcome something you've been told to guard against, especially when you're focused on spreading this so-called "good news." But what's the point of the "good news" if it never really touches us to the bones, gets down in us and revives the dead parts so desperate for their own

Gospel "more". Rhetorical question, obviously, because if it doesn't, then what's the point at all?

TAMING THE UNHAPPINESS

Alright, let's cut to the chase. We're all on this endless hunt for happiness, right? And when we can't find it, we sometimes dive into things we shouldn't—addictions, constant busyness, unhealthy relationships, you name it. Why? Because there's this nagging voice saying, "you're not enough." Been there, done that—I thought being the ultimate good girl in my faith would make me happy. Nope! Just led to resentment.

But here's the kicker: Statistics show that a lot of us women believe damaging lies about ourselves—that we're not good enough, not lovable, not worthy. Those lies we believe, they're like emotional quicksand, pulling us deeper into behaviors we regret. But there's hope, my friend. The moment we let Jesus's authentic love fill those empty spaces in our hearts—that's when we find a happiness that heals, a joy that's so genuine, it's like a soft blanket for the soul.

James put it this way: "What is causing the quarrels and fights among you?... You desire what you don't have, so you scheme and kill to get it. You are jealous of what others have, but you can't get it, so you fight and wage war" (James 4:1-2 NLT). Many of us, particularly those of us with strong religious backgrounds, wage this war internally, stifling our own happiness and potential. We suppress the most vibrant parts of ourselves because our religion tells us we cannot be happy. But life wasn't meant to be this way. **Philosopher Blaise Pascal nailed it:**

"All men seek happiness. This is without exception.

Whatever different means they employ, they all tend to this end…This is the motive of every action of every man, even of those who hang themselves."[3] So, here's the deal. Every one of us is fighting this internal war over happiness, right? Look, no one gets a free pass, not even the "churchy" girls like me who thought they had it all figured out. As a kid, I was basically told that happiness was off-limits. Like, don't even go there. The church said that happiness was for the "worldly" folk, and being the good church girl that I was, I swallowed that line without a second thought.

You'd think the church would be my go-to happy place, right? Wrong. It felt more like I was getting shortchanged. All I heard was "joy this" and "joy that." Now, don't get me wrong. Joy is great, but it felt like the church's safety word. "Joy" was allowed; happiness was not. So there I was, stuck in this confusing limbo between a joy that felt kinda hollow and a happiness I was told was almost sinful. How messed up is that?

Here's the kicker. Deep down, I knew something was off. I had this nagging feeling, this whisper in my soul, telling me not to settle for this sanitized, churchy version of joy. The Bible talked about joy, sure, but it also hinted at a happiness that religion was keeping under wraps. Why settle for watered-down joy when there's this soul-quenching happiness, like what Jesus offered the Samaritan woman? She felt something so emotionally relevant, so GOOD, that she couldn't keep it to herself. She ran to tell the rest of her town. I wanted that. Something so good that I couldn't help but share it with the world!

So what did I do? I finally listened to that inner voice, the one that had been beckoning me to challenge the status quo. I'd been grinding away for years, doing the church thing, and I wasn't getting any of that promised "more." So I decided to rebel, just a little, like Martin Luther shaking up the Catholic Church back in the day. This book, then, is my personal thesis. It's me saying, "No more. You don't get to define my faith or my happiness."

This book is an exposé, y'all. It's about how the church, both modern and traditional, hijacked my happiness and spoon-fed me their own versions of "truth." It's about the years I spent settling for less, thinking that was the "Christian" thing to do. Look, I'm done being a follower, letting other people hold my spiritual hand because I'm too scared to question things. No more settling for second-rate theology or man-made doctrines.

In short, I was spiritually starving while sitting at a feast. I was too afraid to reach for the nourishment only Jesus could provide. But now? Now I'm ready to sidestep the self-appointed religious experts and get my fill straight from the source. And trust me, it's a feast worth attending.

WHAT IS HAPPINESS? AND IS IT BIBLICAL? - A CASE FOR HAPPINESS

Sis, you ready to tap into the good stuff with me? Let's start by examining the term 'joy' as it appears in the Bible. In its original Greek language, 'joy' is translated as 'makario.' This word appears in biblical texts more than fifty times, depending on the translation. Synonyms for 'makario' include 'blessed,' 'joy,' 'happy,' and 'elated.' All emotional states of being! Notably, in 1 Timothy 1:11, the original Greek text speaks of "sound doctrine in accordance with the Gospel of the [makario] that is [happy] God." Yet, in English translations, 'happy' often becomes 'spiritually blessed.'

It's crucial to clarify that the original Greek term 'makario' doesn't point to a nebulous spiritual concept of 'blessedness.' Rather, it directly translates to happiness—a tangible, felt state of well-being. Contrary to traditional teachings, 'joy' and 'happiness' are not that different. 'Joy' in Greek is 'chara,' and it embodies the same sense of elation and gladness that happiness does, a feeling that is felt. They're emotions, meant to be deeply felt and experienced.

Why is this a game-changer? Because it highlights a God who is, in essence, happy. A 'feeling' God. Despite what some religious teachings might say, the Bible tells us God is happy, actually elated. Read 1 Timothy 1:11 again: the Gospel rests on a happy God.

Are you still with me, sis? This is mega important because the Old Testament sets the stage for the New Testament, which ultimately points us to the Gospel. The grand finale is Jesus Christ, who came to erase our sins and bring us back to God's original design—which includes happiness.

If the Old Testament prefigures the New, and the New reveals a Gospel rooted in a 'happy God,' then it's a no-brainer: God wants us happy, girl. No two ways about it. So why do some folks act like happiness is a celestial IOU, only cashable in heaven? If Jesus sought to bring heaven to Earth—and indeed, brought heaven down through His Holy Spirit dwelling in us—then happiness isn't a footnote; it's the headline!

So, why is the pursuit of happiness often stigmatized? Why separate this happiness from the nature of God as if it's a deferred gift to be fully opened only in heaven? If Christ's mission was to bring heaven to Earth, as suggested by His prayer, 'Your will be done, on Earth as it is in Heaven' (Matthew 6:10), then happiness isn't just an afterthought; it's integral to a life aligned with God.

By reframing our understanding of happiness through scriptural and linguistic lenses, we can better appreciate the full scope of God's intentions for us. It's not only about seeking happiness; it's about aligning our lives with the intrinsic happiness of a God who created us for such a purpose to reflect and commune with him! Phew! You get that? That's some Gospel Good News, indeed!

SO WHY SETTLE?

Growing up as good girls in the church, it's easy to feel like we've missed out on the full, vibrant nature of God's happiness. Maybe we don't really know God as well as we think we do. I find it heartbreaking that so many settle for less than what Jesus desires for us, and yet, it also fills me with a sense of purpose to keep advocating for the fuller life Jesus offers.

As we navigate uncharted territory in our faith journey, keep this in mind, my friend: the church isn't the ultimate authority on 'truth.' It's made up of individuals, like you and me, all trying to figure out life and God. And, well, people make mistakes. We don't have to be passive followers; let's be active explorers, stepping onto the less-traveled path that Christ lays out for us.

For too long, I allowed the church to shape my relationship with God. Fearful of "getting it wrong," I trusted imperfect people to guide my faith, leading to pain and brokenness- and therefore much unhappiness. The people I looked up to didn't seem particularly happy themselves; they seemed stern and dire. So, I built emotional walls, allowing my Sunday church experience to barely touch my soul. All this taught me a flawed lesson: that God didn't want me to be happy or full here on earth. But that conclusion was based on my limited experiences, not on the truth of Scripture or the nature of God.

You see, when we sift God's Word through our limited experiences and understanding, we risk reinforcing our preconceived beliefs—whether they're accurate or not. It's human nature to seek validation for what we already think, which can narrow our perspectives. And so, sis, let's get down to the raw, heartfelt truth—I used to think that God was distant, almost robotic—unemotional, unrelatable, untouched, and unfelt. Like my spiritual connection with Him was supposed to be this formal, stilted thing. But, girl, that's changing. The more I dig into the beautiful love story in the Song of Songs and let God romance my soul, the more I understand: God is all about the feels.

In those quiet moments with Him, it's like a light bulb turns on. God is deeply emotional. You know, I've been flipping through the Gospels and seeing Jesus—the human expression of God—in a whole new way. He celebrated. He wept. He even got angry. This is not an emotionally distant God; this is a God who wants to vibe with us on a real, emotional level. To be honest, the idea of an unfeeling God felt wholly unrelatable and, let's just say it, totally unappealing. But here's the real talk: Scripture says that we were made in God's image with hearts that feel, deeply and vividly, to connect with each other, with life's ups and downs, and yes, with God Himself.

This isn't a debate about whether God "allows" us to be happy. This is a revelation: God is emotional, and He's designed us to connect with Him on a deeply emotional level. He doesn't just "allow" our emotions; He created them, and He wants us to experience the fullness of joy, happiness, and every other emotion with Him as the source. Because all that's good—every drop of happiness—flows from Him.

Happiness isn't a trademark of this world. It's a gift from God, and Scripture confirms it: "Every good and perfect gift is from above" (James 1:17). So let's be the daughters of a happy God and reflect that joy and emotional richness that He's planted deep within us. Let's truly live, love, and be happy—just like we were created to do. "Just so, let your light shine before all men, so that they may see your holy lives and give glory to your Father who is in Heaven." Matthew 5:16 (WNT). We're called to be rays of "Sonshine" (yes, pun absolutely intended!) in a world that can sometimes feel so dark and broken. Our mission is to reflect God's radiant beauty in a world that needs Him more than ever. And guess what, sis? It starts with owning that light, that beauty, that 'Sonshine,' within ourselves first. We can't reflect what we don't first have!

Here's the challenge: First, allow yourself to question what you've come to believe. Second, start deconstructing those narratives that have shaped your perception of God, of yourself, and of the happiness you think you're allowed to experience. It might not be easy to challenge these long-held views, but it's essential for owning the happiness rooted in the Gospel. We need to reevaluate and rejuvenate our minds, bodies, souls, and spirits.

Let's really go there and talk about our exhaustion, our pain, and our deep need for Jesus to meet us here and now. Because once we do, we open ourselves up to a fuller, happier life in Him.

LET'S SPILL THE TEA, SIS!

> **Settling for Less?:** Have you ever felt like you're just settling for the bare minimum in your spiritual life, like you're stuck in a spiritual rut? How does that make you feel deep down?

> **God's Vibes:** Do you feel like you've really tapped into God's full range of happiness and good vibes? Or do you feel like you're missing out on something more?

> **Choose Gospel-Happiness:** What's your game plan for leveling up spiritually and grabbing onto that gospel-centered joy? Seriously, what are you waiting for?

> **Lost in Translation:** Were you shook to find out that the OG Greek meanings of words like 'joy' and 'blessed' are way deeper than you thought? How does that change things for you? Does it comfort you that God is deeply emotional?

> **Scripture & Happiness:** Now that you know the original language in the Bible kinda makes happiness and joy BFFs, how does that shift your perspective on what spirituality is all about?

> **Redefining Your Happy Place:** Do you think traditional teachings got it twisted when it comes to finding your happy place? Have you been out there hunting for happiness in the world, when maybe it was right at home in God's embrace all along?

I hope these questions make you take a moment, get all introspective, and truly engage with your faith on a heart level. You deserve a spiritual life that lights you up, girl! 'Feel's and all!

8

OUR FULLNESS IS FOUND IN JEHOVAH SHALOM:
Mind, Body, Soul, Spirit

lright, so real talk. I was at the gym the other day, and you know those super-fit instructors that make you think, "How do they even look like that?" Yeah, one of them had this sign on the door to her office that caught my eye. It said, "Behind every successful woman, is herself." I had to laugh because it's catchy, right? And super aligned with today's "I've got this" vibe. Now don't get me wrong; being your own hype-woman is important. But let's be honest; we're not solely responsible for our own success. Can I get an amen? Sometimes the weight of the world feels lighter knowing that the pressure isn't all on me. So maybe she's all about that 'God's got my back' life, just like us. Or maybe not. Either way, if you live like God's not part of your game plan, you're heading toward a life that might be busy but is ultimately empty. Been there, done that, and it's not a place any of us want to be.

This got me thinking about how much this "I can handle it" mantra influences us. It's like a modern-day echo of what went down with Eve in the Garden. Like a boss babe, she was basically saying, "I got this, God. Step aside. Who needs you?" But that's when things took a nose-dive. Eve ended up sacrificing her inner peace, wholeness, happiness, and basically, paradise. She thought she could have it all, do it all, on her own terms. We've all been there, thinking we don't need anyone, not even God. But the reality is, the moment we think we've got it all under control is often the moment we lose it.

Eve messed up; she turned away from God and opened the floodgates for sin to enter the world. We inherited that legacy, thanks to her. But let's not kid ourselves; we make that same choice pretty much every day when we decide to go solo. We end up losing so much more than we think we're gaining. God came to restore exactly that—everything we lost when we thought we could do it all on our own. The gospel is literally our roadmap back to completeness because it reconnects us to God. Through Jesus, we can rediscover the happiness and wholeness we've been chasing all along. And guess what? God cares deeply about that.

Why? First off, He's our Abba Father, and He is the epitome of goodness (Matt 7:11 ESV). He's all about bringing us back to that state of wholeness that we lost. Secondly, guess what? He is our Jehovah Shalom, the God of fullness, wellness, and peace. Literally, He embodies everything we're searching for.

When God's in His full Trinitarian community—Father, Son, and Holy Spirit—they're complete, and He wants us to experience that same kind of completeness. God in all his parts operate together, not individually. So when we're in sync with our Jehovah Shalom, we can be just as full and complete. Honestly, that sounds refreshing doesn't it? We weren't made to go it alone! But to anchor ourselves in our Big Jehovah Shalom!

SHALOM

Can I share something that was a bit of a game-changer for me? The concept of shalom. You see, English can sometimes fall short in capturing the depth of certain words. Take "love," for example. In English, we have just one word for it, but in Greek, there are four. The same goes for "shalom," which we often translate simply as "peace." But oh, it's so much more than that.

Strong's Concordance (#7965) unpacks "shalom" as completeness, wholeness, health, happiness, peace, and a bunch of other good stuff. And if you think that's interesting, it comes from the root verb "shalam" (Strong's #7999), which carries this whole theme of well-being and prosperity.[4] The Bible mentions "shalom" a whopping 237 times, making it pretty darn clear that God values it highly. So what are we talking about when we say shalom? We're talking about God's deep desire for our happiness, health, prosperity, and, yep, you guessed it, our wholeness.

Here's the kicker: we lost our shalom at the fall. But guess what? God aims to set that right through Jesus. Sure, the world offers its own versions of shalom—think self-care, yoga, meditation, the works. And God can absolutely use these means. But if Jesus isn't at the heart of our shalom, then we're missing out on the real deal. Dr. Shelli Ricci nails it when she says we should see shalom as a force we can "receive and lean into."[5] We gotta break from that "I can do it all" mindset and acknowledge our need for God to fully live our best lives.

Take Romans 16:20, for example: "And God, the source of shalom, will soon crush the Adversary under your feet." Did you catch that? God is our one and only source for true happiness, health, and prosperity. I know, sometimes religious circles make these things sound worldly, but that's far from the truth. These are Godly pursuits because they originated with Him.

Let's not get it twisted. Satan's pretty good at offering counterfeit versions of what only God can provide. Remember how he tried to tempt Eve? Or Jesus after His forty-day fast? We're just as susceptible to these false promises. But, like Jesus, we have the power to resist these traps, through Christ's blood.

Okay, okay. So we're all searching for that perfect state of happiness, wellness, and total 'chill vibe'. But let me spill some truth tea: there are tons of imitations out there pretending to be the real deal, but only God serves the authentic, soul-quenching shalom we crave. I get it, it's so easy to get swept up by the newest self-help trend, or an Instagram guru promising 'enlightenment' in three easy steps. And the thing is, there's always a little sprinkle of truth in there, right? Just enough to make us drop our guard and think, 'Maybe this is it!' But seriously, let's not get it twisted. No amount of yoga, mindfullness, matcha lattes, or inspirational quotes can replace genuine, God-given shalom.

You ever find yourself putting all your trust in some idea or some person, like they've got the blueprint to your happiness? Yeah, we've all been there. And before you know it, you're so deep into it, it's hard to tell God's truth from a really convincing lie. Yikes!

Here's my hope for us: let's dive into God's word, let's educate ourselves and take back our faith. No more settling for half-truths or watered-down wisdom. I genuinely believe that when we get into the nitty-gritty of God's teachings, we'll naturally pull away from anything or anyone who's selling us a counterfeit version of the life God wants for us, whether that's inside the church or outside the steeple.

Are you in? If we stick close to our Jehovah Shalom, trust me, He's got a life of true abundance ready to pour out onto us. A life so full and radiant, it's not just 'Instagrammable,' it's soul-satisfying too!"

A NOTE ON THE LACK OF SHALOM IN RELIGIOUS CIRCLES

Here's something we often sweep under the rug: the missing shalom in our modern evangelical life. I get it, we sometimes shy away from the whole "wellbeing, prosperity, happiness" thing, worried it sounds selfish or too 'worldly' when we're supposed to be spreading the Gospel. But let's not put God's goodness into tiny boxes and then reject them. God wants us to bask in His truth, His goodness, His *everything*, no strings attached.

Honestly, I think we've settled for a strapped-down version of faith that doesn't nourish us as it should. That's why we see so many church leaders who don't exactly walk the Christian talk. The power and peace of Christ haven't transformed their lives in a real, tangible way. Many of us haven't even gotten a whiff of God's genuine shalom.

We're often so cautious, aren't we? We keep God's goodness at arm's length, scared that someone will accuse us of being 'too blessed,' 'too joyful.' There's this unspoken vibe in church that makes us feel like we should be more solemn, more reserved—always focused on the serious task of saving souls, with no time left to simply *be*. But this mindset falls short of the vibrant, Gospel-centered life Jesus promises us.

I want us to rediscover why we first turned to faith. For God's rest, His healing, His promise of a life more abundant. Christ offers a life that doesn't align with the lacking, limited experience many of us know too well. My deepest hope for you, dear sis, is that you grasp this overflowing life Christ has for you.

In earlier chapters, I talked about the four aspects that make up our 'self.' God wants us to enjoy His shalom in every one of these areas: body, soul, spirit, and mind. I've personally lived it and let me tell you, it's transformational. To really get this, sis, we need to plant ourselves, or our metaphorical chair, firmly in Christ and let Him handle the heavy stuff. Lean in, fully surrendered, and watch Him show up big time! He'll guide you in spirit and truth toward healing, and you'll start to feel the depth of His love for you. His love is the ultimate healer. So, whatever your next steps are—be it therapy, daily devotion, repentance, or forgiveness—commit to them. But let's make sure this journey is rooted in Christ, okay? Otherwise, our metaphorical 'house'—or chair—won't stand. Christ is the only foundation we've got. Amen. And over time, this fulfilling sense of shalom will truly be yours. I'm rooting for you, sis! Christ came to radically change our lives, and I want you to experience that transformation—right down to your very core.

LET'S SPILL THE TEA, SIS!

> **You Don't Have to Carry the World, You Know?:** Do you ever catch yourself thinking you can handle everything on your own, without needing anyone, including God? How does that affect your inner peace?

> **Who's in the driver seat?:** We all love that anthem, "Behind every successful woman is herself," but does that ever make you feel kinda isolated? Do you feel the pressure of thinking you are solely responsible for everything? Or do you acknowledge that God is in the driver seat and He is inviting you to come and sit alongside Him through the ultimate road trip of life?

> **What's Your Soul Craving?:** What does the concept of "shalom" mean to you? Do you feel you're experiencing God's intended peace, happiness, and well-being in your life right now?

> **The Insta-Trap:** Are you swayed by trending self-care routines or Instagram gurus promising quick fixes to happiness? How do you discern what truly brings you closer to wholeness?

> **Is Your Faith Feeling Boxed In?:** Have you ever felt that your faith community restricts you from experiencing God's full goodness and shalom? If so, how do you plan on re-aligning your faith to experience a fuller, richer life?

Sit with these for a bit, love. It's in these heart-to-heart moments that we start peeling back the layers that life—and sometimes even church—has piled on us. This is where the healing starts.

9

LET'S TALK SELF-CARE & SELF-LOVE

So, I found myself at a moms' group recently, and the topic? Self-love. My heart soared! Given that I'm penning a book about how religion sometimes distorts the 'self' God wants us to cherish, this felt like a win. "Finally, the church is catching up!" Then the Hillsong track ebbed, and the speaker took the stage. She was a vision with her platinum mini-bun and designer Louis Vuitton saddlebag. We all marveled at her aura of flawlessness. I even caught myself wondering if her eye-catching Maserati was parked outside.

But then the irony unfolded. She kicked off her talk by devaluing 'self-love,' and like wildfire, her skewed ideology caught on. Heads nodded, buying into her twisted 'god-truth.' "Self-love is not rooted in Christ; it's the religion of the godless," she asserted. And there, in that room, countless women were swayed away from self-love—and by extension, self-care.

Here's where we go wrong. This is how we get buried under guilt that should never be ours. This is how we veer toward rigidity, clutching rules over the liberating love of Christ. It's in these moments that we pick up on distorted "truths" from people who should be guiding us toward God's authentic love and grace.

That well-meaning but misguided woman on the stage was actually doing a disservice. She was pushing away the self-care and self-love that we not only deserve but need to function as whole human beings—whole women of God. Her misinterpretation of being 'called to be selfless' creates guilt where there shouldn't be any. It creates boundaries where freedom should exist.

Let's clear the air. Jesus cares deeply about our wholeness, about our self-care, and yes, about our self-love. It isn't about what we can offer to Him or even to others. **The gospel is vital, but it's not just a command to go out and act—it's an invitation to come in and receive.**

Seeking health, wholeness, and self-love isn't a detour from the gospel; it's the embodiment of it! Eve's downfall left humanity broken and incomplete, but Jesus came to reverse that curse. He came to offer us wholeness and completion—to teach us the kind of self-love that fills us up so we can truly love others. The gospel tells the grand tale of God's mission to restore what Eve lost, and we're not just its messengers—we're its recipients.

Embrace self-care. Celebrate self-love. When you do, you're living out the gospel in its most holistic form. You're not only better equipped to serve others but also open to receiving the love God has for you. After all, the most vibrant life in Christ is one where self-care and self-love aren't just welcomed; they're celebrated. **And girl, that's something worth celebrating.**

ARE WE REALLY CALLED TO BE SELF-LESS?

Growing up in an atheistic home didn't offer much hope for a different life path. That changed when a dear grade-school friend introduced me to Christ. Her family's wholesome and joyous home life was evidence enough for me, showing a different life—one I decided to embrace. Soon after, my mom followed my lead and also gave her life to Christ. However, she quickly became consumed with church activities, dedicating hours to volunteering and ministry. Despite her unwavering commitment, she remained as stressed, anxious, and fearful as ever. She had sought spiritual and emotional healing but found only an increasing workload. As a young Christian myself, this wasn't the example I wanted. We both needed a community that could see and value us beyond our capacity for service.

REDEFINING SELFLESSNESS: GOD, SELF-LOVE, AND YOU

So, you know that age-old idea that being 'selfless' is the epitome of faith? Well, let's pause for a real talk moment. When you ignore self-care and self-love, you're not just neglecting yourself; you're actually dismissing God's creation—yeah, that's you!

Science—yeah, good ol' facts—supports self-care and self-love as legit ways to lower stress, boost mental well-being, and even fend off chronic diseases. That's not just trendy self-help jargon; that's maintaining the temple God gave you. And guess what? When you're at your best, you can serve others in a way that's not just going through the motions but truly impactful. Now, I've heard people quote 'not self-seeking' from 1 Corinthians 13:4 as if it's a command to ignore your own needs. Hold up, though! The Greek text, where this all originated, implies that 'not self-seeking' is about avoiding self-centered, me-first behavior. It's not about depriving yourself to the point where you can't serve others effectively.

Let's drop it another way: A pie missing a slice just isn't whole, right? Likewise, when we neglect any aspect of our lives—be it physical, emotional, or spiritual—we're not our whole selves. In the Bible, that's akin to missing out on "shalom," the God-given state of complete health and wellness. Now, let's tie it all together. Science backs up the need for self-care to reduce stress and improve well-being. The Bible doesn't say "neglect yourself"; rather, it warns against selfish, narcissistic behavior. The goal is a balanced, whole life. We're talking about a life that honors God not just in service to others, but also in how we care for ourselves—every slice of that life pie. **That's God's intention. He wants us full, flourishing, and fabulously capable of sharing His love.**

FAITHFULNESS IN THE AGE OF BURNOUT: WHY SELF-CARE ELEVATES OUR SERVICE TO GOD AND FAMILY

Girl, can I just say it? Our churches are losing touch, and we're feeling it. They can seem so disconnected from the nitty-gritty, everyday battles we face. And when we try to set boundaries for our own well-being, why does it suddenly feel like we're being spiritually benched?

Look, our families are our first ministry. They don't need the crumbs of us after we've given our all to every church event, committee, and bake sale. They deserve the whole, well-rounded us. But often, after being the constant 'yes-girl' at church, we're left choosing between our own sanity and giving what's left of us to our families. This is the example of motherhood I saw all around me in the church as a teen, and it never sat well with me.

Time to drop the "yes-woman" act. It's not just about being a people-pleaser; it's about being a God-pleaser. This might mean declining that extra church event to have a family night or maybe even a pampering "me-night." You gotta recharge spiritually, emotionally, and physically.

How to self-care like a pro? Start small. Schedule some God-time every morning—even if it's just 10 minutes. Use that time for gratitude prayers or meditative breathing. Trust me, you'll feel a difference. Set aside time for a hobby you love, like journaling or painting, as an outlet for emotional recharge.

And hey, if you need to take your medicine, schedule that doctor's visit, or therapy session, don't hesitate for a moment. But here's the key: do it all with unwavering trust in God for your healing. He should be the foundation beneath it all. Even when medications or people can't provide the complete remedy, always remember that our Heavenly Father is still in the miracle business, ready to work wonders in your life!

While we're at it, let's talk boundaries. If a church commitment compromises your well-being or takes you away from family, it's okay to say 'no.' If the guilt-trips start, remember your ministry begins at home. Offer to support in ways that are sustainable for you.

And let's not be loners, okay? We need each other. So make a girls' night, share your highs and lows, and lift each other up. Open conversations build stronger, more supportive communities. So here's the low-down, sis: Self-care isn't selfish. It's God's care in action. The better we take care of ourselves, the better we reflect Christ's love and grace to the world. So let's be that church—the one that shows up for each other in every way, no judgment, just love.

SOUL SISTER DISCLAIMER: JUST BETWEEN US AND GOD, OKAY?

Before we tie this whole self-love and self-care package with a bow, let's get something straight, heart-to-heart. We're all on our own journey with God, and let's be honest—our paths are as unique as we are. Some of us have walked through fires that others can't even imagine. This book—especially the parts about self-love and self-care—is like a big, warm hug for anyone who's been through it, okay? Before we wrap up this self-love journey, let's have some real talk. We're all on different spiritual paths, some more winding and rocky than others. And here's the tea: I've heard that some of us tend to see God's love more vividly, while others see more of His wrath. Why? It all comes down to what we've lived through, sis.

If your life's been a bed of roses and you're all about leaning into a more wrathful, just God, that's fantastic—seriously, kudos to you. But let's not throw shade at those who've had a tougher time and need to snuggle into the gentler, more loving side of God, okay? Everyone's journey is unique, sprinkled with trials and tribulations you might know nothing about.

Here's something else—our God is incredibly tailor-made in His love for us. He meets us right where we are, comforting and counseling us in the unique areas we each need. Can we take a moment to praise God for being so absolutely wonderful?

While it's true that some folks, especially in our selfie culture, make an idol out of self-love, that doesn't mean we should toss it out the window. We all need a sprinkle of that love in our lives. And hey, nobody said anything about striving for perfect balance. That just sets us up for a life of rule-following when what we really need is to bask in God's grace.

Sis, let's make a pact. No being spiritual busybodies in each other's lives, alright? Your divine dance with God is yours alone, and who am I to step on your toes?

Remember Job and his so-called 'friends'? They thought they had all the answers and judged poor ol' Job but ended up getting a divine side-eye from God Himself. So let's not be those friends, okay? Let's go for heartfelt prayers, genuine encouragement, and divine love, and keep our noses out of where they don't belong. God's crafting a unique masterpiece in each of us. So, how about we honor that and stand by each other's side? We're all in this intimate dialogue with God, and that's sacred territory, darling. Can we all agree to respect that?

LET'S SPILL THE TEA, SIS!

> **When Faith Feels Like a Burden:** So girl, have you ever felt like faith is all about constant self-sacrifice, even when it takes a toll on your well-being? Does this notion sit well with you, or does it feel kinda off?

> **The Self-Care Debate:** Imagine a spiritual leader in your life saying self-care or self-love is a no-go. How would that make you feel? Would you nod along, or would it stir something up inside you?

> **Church vs. Real Life:** Do you ever feel like the church or religious groups you're part of just don't get the emotional and real-world struggles we go through? Like if it's not super spiritual then it's irrelevant? How does that make you feel?

> **The Power of Saying 'No':** Do you think setting boundaries and turning down commitments sometimes can actually be a self-love move? How can you bring that into your day-to-day, without feeling guilty?

> **Making Room for You, or 'a-hem', God?:** How can you carve out more me-time in your busy life for self-care and loving yourself? What does it look like to include time with the Lord in your self-care routine? God is the only source we can tap into to truly get that self-love and self-care that we all need. Is it time to take a hard look at where you're spending your energy and maybe—just maybe—make a little more room in your life for Him?

10

IT'S TIME TO SET YOURSELF FREE:

When We Get Stuck in the Guilt Trap

66

When we starve our souls of self-love,

we drain the essence of our being.

ey, beautiful souls. Let's have a candid heart-to-heart, as women who often find ourselves as the caregiving heroes in our relationships. How many of us wrestle with the notion that self-care is a selfish act? That we must wear the cape of the ultimate church-girl-superhero, tending to everyone's needs before even considering our own? Trust me, I've walked that path as well. And ya know, Lindsay C. Gibson, who's not just any psychologist but one with over thirty-five years under her belt, really digs deep into this in her book, Adult Children of Emotionally Immature Parents. Trust me, she knows her stuff! (Gibson, 2015).[6]

She opens our eyes to how many of us grow up thinking we have to neglect ourselves to be 'good.' She explains that many of us grow up in households where neglecting our own needs is like a badge of honor. Seriously, if self-sacrifice was an Olympic sport, some of us would have a gold medal in it.

If you're anything like me, you probably soaked up these lessons like a sponge. Like, serving others is good, right? So, the more we do for others, the more we're valued. But here's the deal: real love is not transactional. You don't need to earn it. You are worthy of love and care just because you exist. And that includes love and care from yourself.

We often forget that self-care is NOT selfish. It's self-preservation. We can't pour from an empty cup. Ephesians 5:29 nails it: "For no one ever hated her own body, but instead she nourishes and protects and cherishes it, just as Christ does the church." If that doesn't shout "take care of yourself," I don't know what does.

THE DANGEROUS MYTH: SELF-NEGLECT IN THE NAME OF HOLINESS

Our upbringing, along with church culture, can really warp our self-perception, can't it? How many times have you been told, 'You're just too sensitive,' or been guilt-tripped into doing something you didn't want to? These false guilt traps often linger into adulthood if we don't confront them. And here's the kicker: this can actually cripple our ability to love. Not just others, but ourselves too.

You see, the message we often get from religious circles is that to be holy, we must neglect ourselves. But let's consider God's own example. He's in a triune relationship with Himself—Father, Son, and Holy Spirit. God even declared about Jesus, 'This is my beloved Son, with whom I am well pleased' (Matthew 3:17 ESV). God loves Himself. If God loves Himself, shouldn't we love ourselves too?

So, listen up. Before we can genuinely extend love to others, we've got to accept love—from God and for ourselves. Because, real talk, how you treat yourself is a direct reflection of how you'll treat others. If you're harsh, bitter, and unloving toward yourself, how can you extend authentic love to anyone else? If you're seeking to love like Jesus, start by loving yourself from a deeply personal, God-infused place. Doing this can change not just how you interact with others, but how you interact with yourself, and ultimately, how you interact with God.

Let's tackle another dark corner while we're at it—this idea that neglecting, or even abusing, our bodies can bring us closer to God. Y'all remember that creepy scene in the Da Vinci Code where Silas, that guy who's part of a weird cult, whips himself? Gross, right? But some actually do this in real life, thinking it's a path to holiness. Even the famous Mother Teresa and Pope John Paul II had their own forms of self-denial and self-inflicted suffering. I don't know why but this just shocked me when I read this. I guess because as a girl I always idolized Mother Theresa. I mean we all do. Heck, she was one woman known for her life service to the poorest of the poor! And she received a Nobel Peace Prize for it! I guess it just shook me to realize that even someone so devoted to the Lord could have her own inner struggles to accept God's love outside of what she does. I mean heck! She did it all! And she still struggled to feel loved and worthy and accepted by God!

But let's be clear: Jesus didn't die on the cross so you could continue to punish yourself. His grace is sufficient. You don't need to earn it. We're not supposed to demean ourselves. We're supposed to live in freedom, empowered by the Holy Spirit.

KNOWING THE REAL FROM THE FAKE

Okay, so let's sort out this guilt thing once and for all. There's real guilt, and then there's fake guilt—or what the Bible calls shame and condemnation. Real guilt? That's when we mess up, like gossiping about a friend. It's specific and points us to an area where we can grow and improve. But fake guilt? That's when we feel bad just for existing or for not meeting some impossible standard we or someone else set for us. It's like having what the Bible calls an 'overactive conscience' (1 John 3:20-21 NIV).

Listen up: I want us to pause and soak this in for a moment. If you've welcomed Jesus into your heart, you're covered. Imagine being wrapped in the coziest, softest blanket ever—that's God's love. You're not just safe from God's wrath; you're shielded from His anger through your belief in Christ. It's like being in a spiritual safe zone where no fire can touch you. So, say goodbye to guilt trips about not being 'perfect.' You are worthy of love, from God, from others, and yes, from yourself.

Here's the liberating truth: God is at peace with you. He can't be angry with you. Why? Because all His wrath was poured out on Jesus. You're fully shielded, girl. When God does correct us, it's not out of anger. It's out of fatherly love, aiming to make us more like Christ. And the closer we get to that, the happier and more whole we feel. Why? Because we're aligning with our Maker and our original design. So, if you're feeling that old guilt creeping in when you take a moment for self-care or self-love, shake it off! Caring for yourself isn't selfish; it's actually Godly. Becoming more like Christ means recognizing your worth and embracing His love, both for yourself and for others. Let's stop with the guilt and start with the grace, shall we?

Wanna dig a little deeper? Take a moment and gauge your self-compassion on a scale from 1-10. It'll help you figure out how much you're showing love to yourself. We all need a self-check now and then to make sure we're not trapped in guilt, missing out on the amazing love and freedom that Jesus offers.

Bottom line: If you want to live a gospel-centered life, you've got to include yourself in the love equation. Because loving yourself isn't just okay; it's biblical.

WHY CHRISTIAN WOMEN GET STUCK IN THE GUILT TRAP

1. **Cultural Expectations:** In many Christian communities, there are traditional roles and expectations for women that emphasize caregiving and self-sacrifice. This can create a sense of obligation to always put others first, leading to guilt when focusing on ourselves.

2. **Misinterpretation of Scripture:** Phrases like "take up your cross" and "die to yourself" are often taken out of context and used to support the idea that self-neglect is godly, feeding this cycle of guilt in us religious gals.

3. **Fear of Judgment:** The fear of being labeled "selfish" or "worldly" can lead to a life of extreme self-denial. For some of us, this has been ingrained from a young age through family, community, or religious teachings.

4. **Perfectionism:** Christian teachings often emphasize striving for holiness and moral excellence, which can lead to a cycle of self-

criticism and guilt when us gals feel we're falling short.

5. **Prosperity Gospel Misconceptions:** Some churches teach that happiness and prosperity are signs of God's favor, causing us to feel guilty when we are not experiencing these things. Like "what am I doing wrong if things aren't going right?"

6. **External Validation:** Seeking approval and validation from church members or leaders can make us feel like we always have to do more, leading to burnout and guilt.

7. **Identity Wrapped in Service:** Some of us gals find our identities so tied to our roles in the church and our families that we feel guilty prioritizing ourselves.

BREAK THOSE CHAINS, SIS

If you're on the guilt train, it's time to pull the emergency brake. Constant guilt isn't conviction; it's a red flag that you're buying into a lie. So let's set you free, okay?

WHAT TO DO WHEN GUILT HITS YOU LIKE A TRUCK

◊ **Study the Word, Don't Skim It:** Seriously, did Jesus tell His disciples to burn themselves out? Nope. He invited them to rest and sit at his feet. To dine with him. To enjoy him. To be loved by him. Dive into the Bible and see what it genuinely says about your worth and well-being.

◊ **Learn to Say No, and Say It Clearly:** You're not rejecting people; you're just saying yes to yourself for once. And guess what? That's okay!

◊ **Get Yourself a Girl Gang:** Talk to people you trust, whether it's your sister in Christ or a professional. You don't have to go through this alone

◊ **Mirror Talk:** Look in the mirror and challenge those guilt-inducing thoughts with some truth bombs about God's love and grace. Maybe put some encouraging post-it-notes on your mirror?

◊ **Celebrate Your 'Me Time':** You took a bubble bath and didn't solve world hunger? That's okay! Celebrate the small wins.

◊ **Talk to Someone:** Sometimes, you need more than a bubble bath. If guilt is your constant companion, maybe it's time to seek professional help. And that's totally fine!

◊ **Find Your Tribe:** Surround yourself with folks who get it. A squad that reminds you of your worth and God's grace is the ultimate guilt-buster.

Look, God doesn't deal in guilt; He deals in grace. And as His beautiful, fierce, and gifted daughter, it's time to start dealing in it too. So let's start shaking off those chains of guilt and start living in the freedom God has called you to, sis.

LET'S SPILL THE TEA, SIS!

> **Always the Giver, Never the Receiver?:** You know that feeling when you're always the "go-to" person, like the church's Wonder Woman, but inside you're running on fumes? How's that balancing act working for your soul, love? Are there parts of you that are just yearning to be nurtured? What's the real-life impact on your well-being, your 'chair' so to speak? Are some 'legs' of your chair more wobbly than others?

> **The Worthy-ness Test:** Does love feel like something you've got to win, like a blue ribbon in a life competition? Let's be real: Are you exhausted trying to be "perfect" just to feel like you're enough?

> **Guilt Trippin':** We've all been down that rabbit hole of feeling guilty for, well, basically existing. How has this so-called "false guilt" been a roadblock in your journey to loving and caring for yourself the way that God loves and cares for his own triune God-head? What are some ways you've experienced "false guilt," and how has it affected your ability to prioritize self-care?

> **Mirror, Mirror:** On a scale from 'Self-Critic' to 'Self-Love Queen,' how good are you at treating yourself the way you treat your besties? Where are you skimping out on showering yourself with the love you so freely give to others?

> **Break Free, Beautiful:** What are those 'aha' steps you can take to start releasing that guilt and step into a place of self-love and well-being? After all, you've got to nourish to flourish, darling.

So go ahead, wrap yourself in that cozy blanket and sip that tea, sis. You're not just here to take part; you're here to take in, too. Let's nurture ourselves by getting real for a sec. Shall we?

Part 4:

WHEN YOU'RE READY TO
UNMASK YOUR FAITH

11

BECOMING WELL-WATERED WOMEN OF GOD

So many of us walk through our Christian journey feeling unfulfilled—always giving, but seldom receiving. Our faith often doesn't quench our spiritual thirst, let alone anything else. Trust me, I've been there, and not just in my spiritual life. For as long as I can remember, I've struggled with anemia—a physical condition that leaves me drained and weak when I don't prioritize my well-being. The exhaustion, the headaches, the lightheadedness, and even the thinning hair have been constant reminders that I'm not at my best when I ignore what my body needs.

Just like my physical body can't function properly without the right nutrients, my spiritual life too has felt empty and lifeless when I approached God merely through rituals or strict religious rules. It's like being spiritually malnourished, always thirsty for God's love and practical blessings but never quite satisfied.

THE FALSE PATH OF EXTREME SELF-DENIAL—HOLD UP!

If you've been vibing with me in religious circles, you might have felt like you should put all your needs on the back burner, right? But let's clear the air: extreme self-denial is not the whole story. Jesus wants us to live lives that are not just scraping by, but are bursting with abundance and purpose!

The truth is, God designed us with needs—physical, emotional, and spiritual—and it's not selfish to recognize that. In fact, acknowledging what you genuinely need is the first step toward a fulfilling life in Christ.

How do we become well-watered women, fully nourished in our faith, and capable of nourishing others? Let's dig into that divine well and sip it together, sis.

RECOGNIZE THAT YOUR NEEDS MATTER

Whether you're a young woman navigating your personal faith journey, a new mom wrestling with sleepless nights and endless responsibilities, or someone trying to balance it all, the question remains: what do you need to thrive, not just survive?

We often hear about the basic necessities: food, water, and God. But life isn't that simple, especially when you're juggling multiple roles. Your happiness matters. Your emotional health matters. Your dreams and aspirations matter. Knowing and attending to these needs doesn't make you any less Christian; it makes you fully human, which is how God created you to be.

BUILD A STRONG FOUNDATION

To grow as well-watered women, we need a solid foundation. For us, that foundation is Jesus Christ. As the Bible says, "For no one can lay any foundation other than the one already laid, which is Jesus Christ." (1 Corinthians 3:11 NIV). Once our roots are firmly planted in Him, we can start to grow and reach for the nourishing light, meeting our needs through His grace.

AN ALL-ENCOMPASSING FAITH: COLLABORATE WITH GOD TO MEET ALL YOUR NEEDS

We're multi-faceted beings—body, mind, soul, and spirit—and God calls each part "very good." Our faith should touch every aspect of our lives. Yes, we have spiritual needs, but we also have emotional and physical needs. We require rest, good food, fellowship, and boundaries. As women, we also have a desire to dream, plan, and collaborate with God on this beautiful adventure called life.

The Proverbs 31 Woman? Yea, her. She's not just spiritually focused; she's also savvy, capable, and knows the value of self-care. She's the OG well-watered woman, nourishing herself to nourish her community. She's thriving in every season because she's aligned herself with God's wisdom in all areas—health, relationships, and even business.

For real, we can take a leaf out of her book. You know the saying, "You can't pour from an empty cup." It's so true. We need to fill our own cups first—spiritually, emotionally, and physically—before we can pour into others. There you have it, sis. A well-watered woman is a well-rounded woman. She leans on God, takes care of herself, and is then fully equipped to show up for others. So let's start meeting ALL our needs in collaboration with God, and watch how we thrive, okay? Amen to that!

THE RIPPLE EFFECT: IT STARTS WITH YOU!

Imagine the impact we could make if we lived as well-watered women—women so full of God's love and grace that we naturally overflow, nourishing those around us. Your kids, your spouse, your community could all benefit from the spiritual abundance flowing from your life. And isn't that the best kind of gospel outreach? As we find our fulfillment in Christ, we become living testimonies of His goodness, drawing others toward the same life-giving well.

We need to prioritize our well-being, not as an act of selfishness, but as an essential part of our Christian journey. Let's be women who not only know how to pass on God's blessings but also how to receive God's blessings. It's time to stop feeling spiritually drained and start becoming well-watered women of God.

UNDERSTANDING OUR GOD-GIVEN NEEDS: A FRESH LOOK AT MASLOW'S HIERARCHY—YAY!

Okay, okay. So we all have needs, right? Yea, we get it. But oh my stars, the definitions of these needs can vary like day and night depending on who's talking! Some folks might say we only really need water, food, and God. Essential, of course, but come on, there's a whole world of other stuff our souls are craving!

So, what's the typical answer when we ask folks what they need to live their best lives?

> Happiness (Who doesn't want to be happy?!)
> Health (Amen to that!)
> Family (Our forever crew!)
> Dreams fulfilled (Check!)
> Community of girlfriends (Yep! We need our gals!)
> Creative expression (Umm y'all, who doesn't love a little sparkle in life?!)

Guess what, lovelies? The divine news is, you don't have to pick and choose between these fabulous needs and living a Gospel-glowing life. Get this: acknowledging and meeting your needs doesn't take you away from God; it brings you closer to Him and the full, vibrant life He wants for you!

A PSYCHOLOGICAL PERSPECTIVE ON NEEDS—NOT JUST BRAINY STUFF!

Alright, let's talk Maslow! Ever heard of Abraham Maslow, the brilliant psychologist? He gave us this super insightful hierarchy of human needs that's basically a roadmap for life (see next page).

Now, in some churchy settings, the vibe is often about just covering the basics—think psychological, safety, and social needs. These are those 'deficiency needs' as seen in the diagram. Super important, but darling, we are destined for so much more! The higher you climb Maslow's fabulous pyramid to reach those higher needs, the closer you get to becoming your most radiant self! How awesome is that?

A FRESH TAKE ON HIERARCHY OF NEEDS—WITH A SPRIN-KLE OF FAITH!

Flip the page and you'll see I've given Maslow's chart of needs a fresh spin. I've had so much fun reimagining Maslow's hierarchy to better align with our faith, y'all! But here's a twist: let's add in our foundational spiritual needs, the bedrock that supports all the other layers. Prayer, scripture, community, worship—these are our spiritual 'vitamins,' if you will. They're as essential as air, giving life to our souls and purpose to our journey. From that foundation it continues to grow upwards-physiological, safety, social, self-esteem, cognitive,

SELF-ACTUALIZATION

AESTHETIC NEEDS

COGNITIVE NEEDS

SELF-ESTEEM NEEDS

SOCIAL NEEDS

SAFETY NEEDS

PHYSIOLOGICAL NEEDS

SPIRITUAL NEEDS

GROWTH NEEDS

DEFICIENCY NEEDS

aesthetic, and self-actualization, which brings us to full transcendence. Now, we don't have to get into all that mumbo jumbo, but the ideas still stand: the more wholly our needs are met, the more fulfilled, whole, and beautiful our lives become.

Let's break it down, sis! Building upwards from our spiritual foundation, we've got physiological needs—food, water, sleep. Ever read about Jesus multiplying the loaves and fishes? He was meeting physiological needs so that folks could focus on spiritual ones. God wants us to nourish ourselves physically so that we can be strong in our faith journey.

Next, we got safety. Think about it like this—God as our ultimate protector, provider, our rock, and fortress. Feeling secure and safe allows us to be emotionally available to connect with God and others.

On to social needs. God created us for fellowship, right? Scripture tells us to love our neighbor, and being socially connected helps us to better emulate Christ's love.

Ah, self-esteem! God doesn't want us drowning in insecurity; He made us in His image, so let's own that, girl! Our self-worth comes from Him, not likes on social media.

Cognitive and aesthetic needs? Well, that's where our faith gives life color and dimension. Like appreciating a stunning sunset or engaging in thought-provoking Bible study—our minds and souls flourish when these needs are met.

And hey, self-actualization is the whipped cream and the cherry on the top- the stuff you don't wanna go without! When we dive into self-actualization, it's like syncing up with God to dream big dreams and chase those dreams like there's no tomorrow. Imagine being so aligned with God that you're not just existing, but passionately moved to co-create a life of purpose with Him—just like Esther, who recognized she was born for 'such a time as this.'

> WHAT ARE SOME OF YOUR DREAMS? HOW CAN THESE DREAMS LEAD YOU INTO MORE INTIMACY WITH OUR DREAM-GIVER?

This is where it all blends together beautifully. It's about a vibrant conversation with God, where you bring your imagination, hopes, and even your fears to the table. He listens, He responds, and together you sketch out a divine blueprint. You become an active participant in His grand design, co-authoring your story with the Author of Life.

Sound good? This is not just about dreaming; it's about bringing those dreams to fruition. It's like partnering with God, our ultimate Dream Giver, to not only dream but to actually see those dreams manifest. This is about moving mountains together, not just standing there looking at them. So, unlock your full potential for kingdom impact and let your heart soar. Dream big, because God is big, and He wants to do big things through you!

Finally, let's chat about that transcendence Maslow mentions. In faith terms, this is about becoming so aligned with God's will that we're not just living, but thriving in a way that brings glory to Him. It's about stepping into the fullness of who God designed us to be, echoing what Jesus said in John 10:10, "I have come that they may have life, and have it to the full."

Transcendence is that moment when your spiritual gifts, talents, and passions intersect to serve not just you, but the Kingdom. It's feeling God's pleasure when you're in that "zone." It's kind of like when Peter stepped out of the boat onto the water—defying all logic and simply trusting. That's transcendence, darling. And it's available to all of us who seek a deeply rooted, unwavering relationship with God.

So let's aim for it, shall we? Aim to live lives so rich, so full, that we transcend the everyday and touch the divine. Because that's where the real magic—no, the real miracles—happen. So there it is, y'all. Understanding Maslow's hierarchy with a dash of faith reminds us that our needs—physical to spiritual—are interconnected, and God wants to meet every single one. Let's lean into that and live our most fulfilled lives, shall we?

A GOSPEL-CENTERED APPROACH TO LIVING FULLY—SAY IT WITH ME: AMEN!

Here's the low-down: God made us wonderfully complex! We're called to meet all these exciting needs, not just the basic ones- starting from the bottom and building one-by-one all the way to the top. Whether you're thirsting for creative expression, meaningful relationships, or understanding your God-given purpose, these yearnings are in you for an amazing reason! Living life Gospel-centered means we're gunning for total enrichment: spiritually, emotionally, mentally, and you bet, physically too! In doing so, we become a blessing factory: to God, our families, our communities, and guess what? Ourselves!

So, put on those spiritual running shoes and let's dash into the full life God has in store! This is your VIP invitation to be well-watered women of God: fulfilled, purposeful, and ready to sprinkle blessings everywhere we go!

ARE YOU GETTING YOUR DAILY SOUL SIPS? LET'S TALK

SPIRITUAL HYDRATION!

Here's the tea, yea, Maslow had this very practical hierarchy of needs. But let this be a reminder, girl. Before we even dream of climbing that pyramid, we need our foundation to be as solid as a rock. And not just any rock, but the Rock, Jesus Christ! Preach it, 1 Corinthians 3:11: "For no one can lay any foundation other than the one already laid, which is Jesus Christ" (NIV). Can I get an Amen?!

From Genesis to Revelation, Jesus is the cornerstone, darlings! Isaiah 28:16 shouts it loud and clear: "Therefore thus says the Lord GOD, behold, I am the one who has laid as a foundation in Zion, a stone, a tested stone, a precious cornerstone, of a sure foundation" (ESV). A firm foundation in Christ? Sis, that's like spiritual Wi-Fi— connection secured! So, stay connected to your Source daily, and you'll soon bloom into a well-watered, fully transcendent woman of God!

BE CAUTIOUS OF RELIGIOUS ROADBLOCKS—YIKES!

Sadly, darlings, religious circles can be like, "Hold up, you're aiming too high!" They might guilt you for wanting too much from life and expecting too much of God. But here's the thing: God's love and blessing isn't limited, and neither should our lives be. We don't serve a God of scarcity but a God of abundance! The world outside may have it half-right, meeting needs without the ultimate Foundation, but we have the whole package! It's time to dive deep into God's over-flowing river of grace. Imagine that river flowing within you, cutting through dry places and nourishing every part of your life.

YOUR LIFE AS A LIVING TESTIMONY—GIRL, LET'S GLOW!

HOW WELL AM I BEING *watered* ?

rate the level which each need is being met on a scale of 1 to 5

SPIRITUAL NEEDS

Spiritual essentials include cultivating a close and personal relationship with God through consistent time in His presence. Trusting God's good plans for you, embracing the freedom and inner healing that come through Christ, and seeing the fruits of the Spirit manifest in your life as a testament to your status as God's cherished child.

SAFETY NEEDS

Stability in employment, well-being in health, and the sanctuary of a secure home—these are God-given provisions we all need, given to us by our Heavenly Father.

SELF-ESTEEM NEEDS

Grounding your self-worth in God's love for you, cultivating Christ-like courage, and treating yourself with the same compassion that Jesus shows us—this is the essence of divine confidence and self-assurance.

SELF-ACTUALIZED GOAL

Embrace a sense of self that is unashamed and rooted in Christ, while understanding your God-given potential and worth. Tap into your full potential, knowing it's God who's empowering you to be all you can be. Be curious and open about life, yourself, and others, all while growing stronger in your relationship with God."

PHYSIOLOGICAL NEEDS

Essential needs include clean air, water, food on the table, some cute outfits, and a cozy space to call home. Never underestimate the importance of these basics in your life!

SOCIAL NEEDS

Life is so much better with our tribe. Prioritize your friendships, family, and community. They're not just a nice-to-have; they're a must-have.

COGNITIVE NEEDS

Growing in wisdom and truth, developing personal convictions, fostering curiosity and exploration.

AESTHETIC NEEDS

An appreciation for and inclusion of beauty, balance, organization, order, and cleanliness.

TRANSCENDENCE NEEDS

Realizing you're a small piece in this big, beautiful puzzle called life. It's that deep-down desire to give back, not because you have to, but because you want to make the world a better place. It's about using those God-given talents and passions of yours to spread some love and light.

I'm living proof, gals! I'm not who I was twelve years ago. I'm better, whole, happy, free, and so much more—all thanks to God! He's that amazing! Just like God watered me, He can do the same for you. Trust in His good plans, and girl, you'll bloom! Let's become Gospel-centered gals who thrive, not just survive! No more playing small for Jesus. We're meant to be like lush gardens, not just potted plants. Let's become so well-watered in Christ that we can't help but nourish everyone around us.

Imagine that! Living billboards for Jesus, not the religious statue kind but the kind filled with the Spirit and life! The people in our lives will be like, "Girl, what's your secret?" And we'll point them straight to the Source—Jesus! (1 Peter 3:15 ESV).

LET'S DO THIS, BEAUTIES!

Come on, let's bring the same love and energy we'd share on a missions trip or church outreach to our own souls. Forget about the rigid rules and judgment. Instead, let's create authentic connections with ourselves, others, and God. We're talking real, genuine, from-the-heart connections that will be a living, breathing Gospel message to the world! Cheers to becoming well-watered women of God!

LET'S SPILL THE TEA, SIS!

> **Spiritual Greenhouse or Just Decor:** What does being a "well-watered woman of God" mean to you? Are you flourishing in a spiritual greenhouse or just a decorative plant in the corner? How different is that from just clocking in and out of church activities like it's a 9-5 job?

> **Your Cup Runneth Over?:** Let's talk about emotional and physical needs—have you ever felt like you've been putting those on the back burner, thinking that's what God wants? You are a whole person, wonderfully made. How can you balance your emotional, physical, and spiritual well-being while still keeping Christ at the center?

> **From Potted Plant to Flourishing Garden:** Ever feel like your spiritual life is more akin to a potted plant on life support than a lush, thriving garden? What specific nourishment do you need right now? How can you turn to God to water those dry areas?

> **Finding Vibrance Through Christ:** How could letting Christ into every corner of your life—not just the Sunday-morning corners—bring you closer to that vibrant, full life He has planned for you?

> **Ripple Effect:** Ever thought about how your personal spiritual wellness could spill over to bless your community, your family, and your friendships? You thriving could be the start of a whole wave of goodness. (We'll chat more about this in Chapter 18, but for now brainstorm just a little, sis.)

Grab your cuppa, sister, because this is where the soul-deep conversations start.

12

HEY GIRL, LET'S TALK ABOUT THE REAL DEAL IN FAITH

Can we have a real chat? Life's got you doing the most—between changing diapers, being the rock-star wife, or juggling your job and your studies. And oh, let's not forget the ever-looming "be a Proverbs 31 woman" goal hanging over our heads. You too? Yeah, thought so.

It feels like you're supposed to be this picture-perfect Christian woman, but deep down, you're like, "Who even am I anymore?" Same, sis. Same. We get so caught up in roles and rules that we forget there's a simple, heart-centered faith we once had.

Remember those youth group days, where a simple worship song could move you to tears? When praying didn't feel like a chore, but like you were chatting with your best friend? What happened to that?

I'm here to spill some truth tea: You didn't lose it. It got buried under religious to-dos and what-not-to-dos. But God's not about checklists, and neither is real faith. So how about we do something radical? Let's take it back.

No, seriously, let's go back to basics. It's time to put down the religious rulebook and pick up grace. Because if you're feeling lost, you're not going to find yourself in another church bake sale, sis. You're going to find yourself where you left her—on her knees, in prayer, filled with awe and wonder for a God who loves you just as you are.

Look, God doesn't want you to lose yourself in the process of loving Him or others. Your quirks, your dreams, and yes, even your Pinterest fails—they all make you, YOU. And God loves YOU.

This is your wake-up call. Maybe it's time to trade the 'shoulds' for some 'coulds.' Instead of saying, "I should be doing this," maybe start saying, "I could do this to get closer to God and be a better me."

I want us to stop running the rat race and start running our own race—our faith journey. Let's reclaim that joy, that child-like wonder, that makes every day with God an adventure. And you better believe, when we're living out our true selves, we become better moms, better wives, and most importantly, better daughters of God. Are you with me?

THE NARROW ROAD

This journey towards a genuine gospel life has been my lifeline. I used to think that being a Christian meant nailing my true self to the cross just to feel worthy in God's eyes. Yeah, I thought the gospel was this calling to go so deep into selflessness that I'd lose all my quirks, all my feels—like, ALL of me.

But if I'm being honest, that path was not just making me lose my sparkle; it was killing my soul. And not in a "take up your cross" way, but in a "who am I anymore?" way. I was trading in everything that made me feel alive, vibrant, and connected to something so much bigger than myself. All the little and big joys that made my heart sing? Gone. And for what? A religious fight that was never mine to fight in the first place. Girlfriend, spoiler alert: Jesus already won that battle.

It's like I took a wrong turn and left the narrow road, the one where little me walked hand-in-hand with Jesus, full of childlike wonder. Instead, I found myself stumbling down this rocky, twisted path that was just religion disguising itself as faith. And let me tell you, that path? It didn't care about the real me. The vulnerable, messy, dreaming me got bruised and beaten by every stone and thorn on that way.

So now, I'm reclaiming that narrow road. Because it's time to walk with Jesus in a way that doesn't make me leave myself behind. Are you with me, sis? Because the best version of you is the one that God created, and she is glorious.

REDISCOVERING THE NARROW PATH TO HIM

Deconstructing my faith and constructing an authentic relationship with God has been so important to me. For the longest time, I thought being a good Christian woman meant burying the real me to make room for what I thought was a 'holy' version of myself. And I'm not just talking about your average sacrifices—no, I went all in, thinking I had to be this perfect person to earn God's love. It was as if I was saying goodbye to my very essence, you know, the part of me that made me feel connected to God in the first place.

I know I'm not alone; maybe you've felt this too? Like you were so caught up in the rules and rituals that you lost sight of God's love and grace? Like the religion you were practicing was more of a battleground than a sanctuary? This all-or-nothing mentality had me trading in my God-given passions and joys for a list of 'dos and don'ts.' It felt like I was erasing parts of myself for a battle that—let's be real—has already been won by Jesus.

I had to look back and see how I'd strayed from that narrow road of genuine faith I once knew so well as a young girl. You know that time in your life when the simple act of picking a daisy could make your whole day, or when your biggest adventure was climbing a tree? When you were excited about pink milk and painting your toenails?

But adulthood, am I right? It's like we suddenly hit this phase where we're supposed to have it all together, where life gets 'serious,' and we risk losing that sense of wonder. Honestly, my religion played a big part in fast-tracking that loss. As if being an adult means you've got to give up the joy, creativity, and spontaneity that God so loves in us. And for what? To earn something? Prove something? What am I beating myself up for?

Here's the truth: chasing after God through the lens of rigid religion not only distances us from our true selves but also takes us miles away from God's heart. It's like that moment in The Hobbit when Gandalf warns Frodo before entering Mirkwood, "Keep your eyes on the path. For once you lose it, you'll never find it again." And let me tell you, the path back to God, back to who He created me to be, has been an ongoing journey—but it's been worth every single step.

NAVIGATING THE FORESTS OF FAITH

You know how life feels like a wilderness sometimes? Like you're in your own version of Mirkwood, battling invisible fears and searching for something more—love, meaning, a deeper connection with God. Well, that's been my journey, too. The tricky part? Religion often whispers, "You can't have all that. You're selfish for even wanting it." But hey, don't be fooled. Sometimes, those guiding us in the church may also be a bit lost.

Remember the zeal you had when you first met Jesus? You knew you were on this amazing narrow path with Him. But then religion came along, offering an easier, wider route that seemingly held your hand and gave me the supposed cliff notes on how to be close to God. Let's be honest, I took it. And it led me far from the authentic faith I had as a child, far from the "me" I used to be and miss so much. So here I am, back on the narrow path, still healing from the emotional scars and unpacking the misleading narratives I picked up along the way.

FINDING THE REAL MEANING OF LIFE: UNPACKING WHAT JESUS REALLY MEANT BY 'THE WORLD'

You're likely familiar with the cautionary words of Jesus in Mark 8:36: "For what does it profit a man to gain the whole world and forfeit his soul?" A wakeup call if there ever was one, right? But here's the snag—some religious leaders have co-opted the concept of the 'world' to label anything 'unspiritual' as off-limits. However, I'm here to say: that's not the full story.

When Jesus speaks of the 'world,' He isn't asking us to relinquish our joy, creativity, or the simple pleasures that make life worth living. Rather, His warning is against a life void of the richness He desires for us—a life of cluttered up treasures and mired religious legalism that estranges us not only from our authentic selves but also from God, the very One we're striving to please.

What I've learned is that the term 'world'—as used throughout the Gospels—refers to any teaching or lifestyle incongruent with the abundant life that Jesus offered through His death and resurrection. "Worldy" OR religious. We can tend to get pretty preachy about the obvious sins and miss the big ol' elephant in the room all because it's wrapped up in a big ol religious bow. Sometimes those in the church are so much farther from God than those of the "world". And you'd never know it from first glance.

It's crucial to note that much of Jesus' ministry was aimed at the religious, against whom He preached rigorously. In the religious landscape of His time, the Pharisees, Sadducees, and other religious leaders embodied the very 'world' Jesus advised His followers to avoid. Their hearts, by and large, were far removed from God's. Unfortunately, those same religious guys lost their own souls in the process because they rejected Christ. They formed the religious "world" Jesus warned against.

So, let's not mince words: man-made religious rules are not only diverting us from a genuine experience of God, but they're also depriving us of the vibrant, fulfilling life that the Gospel promises. And isn't that the life we're all yearning for deep down? A life not just mired in ritual, but genuinely overflowing with purpose, love, and an intimate connection to our Creator.

FROM RUNNING ON EMPTY TO LIVING ON FULL: REDISCOVERING OUR AUTHENTIC SELVES ON THE NARROW PATH

The journey of faith is often mistaken as a journey of rules— man-made constructs that tell us what we can and can't do, what we should and shouldn't love. In the days of Jesus, these legalistic pathways led even religious leaders to crucify the Savior they claimed to wait for. Shockingly, their religious world and our religious world are not much different. Just as they put their Savior on a cross, so have we, in lesser ways, hung our true selves on a cross of false piety, rules, and hustle.

But let's rewind for a moment. Remember that critical verse in Mark 8:36? "What does it profit a man to gain the whole world and forfeit his soul?" Whether it's the secular world's glamor or the religious world's rigidness, both can lead us away from God, making us lose sight of who we were created to be. And that's the crux of it all—being allied with either world is a betrayal of our true selves and a separation from God.

In an aim to escape the discomfort within, we've sprinted away from our true selves, ignoring the fearful cries of our inner child. Yet, in the haste to 'arrive,' we've ignored the fact that the race is unending and increasingly isolating. I've been there, too—consumed by the religion of busyness and perfectionism, so much so that my soul felt like it was on life support.

But there's good news: we can find our way back to the narrow path. It's not about striving, but about surrendering. It's about sitting in stillness until we feel God's presence saturate our anxious souls, guiding us back to our authentic selves, the little girl inside each of us yearning to be set free.

I've stepped off the broad road that promised me everything but gave me emptiness, and I've tasted that forbidden apple adorned with "self-sufficiency" labels. I've felt that crushing defeat at the road's dead-end. Yet, that was where I found my way back to the narrow path that leads to fullness of life—where love, peace, simplicity, and authenticity reign.

This is my invitation to you to return to these sacred spaces within us, to be truly present in the lives we're building, not just for ourselves but for our friends, families, and communities. Let's allow ourselves to be guided by the love and wisdom that can only come from an intimate relationship with God. Let's not just exist, but truly live. Let's join in again amongst the living of the world and enjoy that which the Lord has made and called "oh so good".

LET'S SPILL THE TEA, SIS!

> **Life Isn't a Spiritual To-Do List:** Let's be real, girl. Faith isn't a checklist; it's an ever-evolving relationship with our deeply romantic and big God. How does that truth make your heart feel different about your spiritual walk?

> **When Rules Become Walls:** Have you ever felt like religious rules are walls separating you from God's love? What could melt those walls and let the love flow in?

> **The Simplicity of Child-Like Faith:** Remember the last time you felt a pure, uncomplicated connection with God, like the innocence of a child? What stole that simplicity from you, and how can you bring that sacred simplicity back into your heart?

> **Lost and Found—Your Inner Sparkle:** When did you feel like you lost a piece of your soul's sparkle because you were trying so hard to be "perfect" in your faith? How can you use this loss as a connection point with your good and perfect Father, God and recover that lost shimmer?

> **Living Authentically and Abundantly:** We know Jesus wants us to have an incredible life full of love and purpose. So, what's one small step you can take to bring your heart closer to that dream, free from what society or your church tells you should do?

> **Is Legalism Your World?:** What's your take on the concept of the 'world' as mentioned in this chapter? Jesus directs much of his teaching against the Pharisees and religious leaders of his time, do you agree that religious legalism can also be a form of 'worldliness' that distracts from an authentic relationship with God?

Feel free to journal these, or better yet, make them your next deep convo topics with your girls. Getting real about these questions could be your next spiritual game-changer.

13

BUILDING AN ATTACHMENT TO GOD:

Breaking Down the Walls and Finding Wholeness

H ey there, lovely ladies! So, as I sit down to share this chapter with you, I'm thinking about a major spiritual crossroads that seriously stumped me for years. Have you ever felt like you're just going through the motions in church, hearing about a God that you should trust but somehow can't? Like you're stuck in a rut? Trust me, I've been there too—especially as a young woman navigating life's twists and turns, and later as a mama with an ever-expanding to-do list.

Here's my story. I knew deep down I needed God for true healing and wholeness. I wanted to trust Him, really, I did. But the God I heard about from the church pew? Better yet the God I'd sifted through my own life's experiences and heartache? He didn't seem all that trustworthy. My heart had built up these towering walls, ya'll, keeping God—and honestly, most people—at arm's length. For heaven's sake, I trusted God for salvation, but trusting Him with my daily life? That was a whole other story.

Now let's bring some psychology into the mix. Have you heard of attachment theory? It's like baby 101: we cling to our caregivers and gauge safety based on those early bonds. But what happens when those early bonds aren't all that secure? Fast forward, and we're grown women projecting those same insecurities onto God.

This is what changed for me: I prayed a desperate, raw prayer: "God, you claim to be good, but I need to see it to believe it. Help me know you differently." And guess what, sis? He answered. God started chipping away at my emotional fortress, brick by brick. Little by little, He revealed Himself as someone entirely different from the God I thought I knew—the God I'd heard about from the pulpit.

Y'all I hope you're catchin' what I'm spillin': this isn't just about surface-level self-care, it's about deep soul-care. Correcting the way we relate to our glorious God is the answer to correctly establishing the foundation to a healthy, happy, and whole YOU! If we can tear down these walls of untrust, we'll find that behind them is a God who wants us to be wholly us—fully healed, and genuinely happy, no checkboxes needed. Let's let Him in and truly live in His love, shall we?

THE HEART OF DIVINE ATTACHMENT: BUILDING YOUR ANCHORED CONNECTION WITH GOD

Darling, whether you're acing exams, navigating married life, juggling motherhood, or embracing singleness—pause and take a deep breath. This chapter is like a warm cup of tea for your soul, crafted just for you. We're diving into a subject that's universal, profoundly transforming, and applicable no matter where you're at in life: attachment. And not just any attachment, but our attachment to God Himself. While John Bowlby and Mary Ainsworth laid the groundwork with their attachment theory, I've been inspired to put my own spin on it, focusing on our attachment with God, Himself.

While reading 'The Connected Parent,' an enlightening book by Dr. Karyn Purvis, it hit me: at the core of every meaningful relationship is an attachment founded on trust (Purvis et al., 2020).[7] Now, before you think this is only applicable to earthly relationships, let's take a heavenly detour. Think about your relationship with God. Isn't it the same principle? He longs for us to trust Him so that a deep, unbreakable attachment forms, one where we feel safe, valued, and endlessly loved.

Why is attachment such a big deal? Well, when we build this kind of relationship with God, it not only strengthens our faith but also empowers us in our earthly relationships. Just like a child who forms a healthy attachment learns self-worth, self-assurance, and emotional balance, we too, when securely attached to God, find our spiritual and emotional footing.

Dr. Karyn Purvis, Lisa Qualls, and Emmelie Pickett, the souls behind 'The Connected Parent,' speak to our hearts when they say attachment feels like a warm hug for your soul. It whispers, 'You're safe, sweetheart. You matter. When you call or need something, someone you love will always show up'.

Isn't this true for our divine relationship as well? In the arms of God, we find the ultimate "Yes." He assures us that we're precious in His eyes and that our prayers—our spiritual cries—are heard. When we seek Him genuinely, He always shows up, tearing down any walls we've built around our hearts.

So, to all my girls out there, whether you're just starting to explore your faith or you've been walking with God for years, know that the concept of attachment is as real in heaven as it is on earth. The more you open up to God, lean on Him, and allow Him to meet your innermost needs, the more you'll experience the fullness of His love and the richness of a life lived in divine attachment with your Creator, your tender-hearted Father, God. It's a journey of deepening trust and love, one where you don't just exist but truly, passionately live—both in your relationship with God and others. Let's strive for that, shall we?

THE SEASON OF DIVINE YESES: HOW GOD'S AFFIRMATIONS SHAPE OUR FAITH JOURNEY

Let's continue our soulful conversation about attachment, but with a celestial twist. You may be familiar with the term "the season of yeses" from early childhood psychology. During the first couple of years of a child's life, her world is shaped by the word "yes." Yes to late-night feeding. Yes to cuddles and lullabies. Yes to everything she needs to grow and feel loved. This season is fundamental in forming a child's sense of self and her attachment to her caregivers. But did you know this parallels our own spiritual journey, too?

Imagine God as the Ultimate Parent during your spiritual "season of yeses." He's there saying, "Yes, I hear your midnight prayer." "Yes, I'll comfort you in your anxiety." "Yes, I'll guide you when you're lost." "Yes, I'll give you peace in chaos." "Yes, I love you unconditionally." By answering these spiritual cries, God is establishing a secure attachment with us. He's showing us not only that our needs are valid but that we ourselves are infinitely valid in His eyes.

As we experience His unwavering yeses, our trust in God deepens. We attach ourselves more securely to Him, paving the way for a life filled with divine love, guidance, and incredible emotional and spiritual well-being.

Whether you're a busy mom, a career-driven woman, or a student trying to juggle it all, take a moment to consider the divine yeses you've experienced in your life. These yeses from God are the building blocks of your spiritual journey, shaping you into the faith-filled woman you're becoming. Every time God says "yes" to us, He's nurturing our spiritual growth, validating our existence, and deepening our faith. He is our Abba Father and He longs to give us good gifts (Matt 7:11 ESV). Let's cherish those beautiful yeses and allow them to lean us into a deeper relationship with God. After all, we're not only His daughters but also the very apple of His eye.

UNPACKING THE SPIRITUAL PARALLEL: GOD AS THE PERFECT CAREGIVER

It's true, not everyone grows up with a fairy tale home life. In fact, some of us were raised in families that were far from perfect. Maybe there was neglect, detachment, or straight-up abuse. If that's your story, you're far from alone. I think we can all nod our heads at the saying, "Hurt people, hurt people." Sad but true. If you grew up in an environment where trust was a scarce commodity, it's easy to project that same detachment onto your relationship with God. Everything might feel transactional, emotionally distant, or even intimidating. But can I share something mind-blowing? Your connection with God, at its core, is relational. He's the ultimate Parent—our heavenly Father—and He's into attachment just like we are. So, if you feel like you missed out on those "Yes Seasons" of attachment in your early life, take heart! God's in the business of filling voids and healing brokenness. He's all about giving you what you didn't get in those early years, and even more.

You see, the need for attachment doesn't expire when you hit adulthood. Far from it! Those early hurts, they're kind of like emotional baggage that we don't even realize we're carrying. But as we grow older, we can't ignore them anymore. Whether or not we had solid attachments in childhood, we all desperately need to form a strong, positive attachment to God. That's the attachment that ultimately heals, sustains, and empowers us.

Let's break it down. To form a heartfelt and authentic bond with Christ, you've got to believe, really believe, that He's in your corner. And this belief isn't something that you can just will into existence. It comes from consistently experiencing God meeting your needs and the longings of your heart. That's why Jesus told us to approach Him like little children—open, needy, and trusting. We need to open our hearts to Him, invite Him into our needs, ask Him in faith, and keep asking in faith until He answers. And He always always does when we ask with expectant and undoubting hearts. Because more than anything He wants us to know we're cherished and valued, not just as a theological idea but as a lived experience. This is the foundation upon which we can build a dynamic, unwavering trust in Him through all the highs and lows of life.

"Ask, and the gift is yours. Seek, and you'll discover. Knock, and the door will be opened for you. For every persistent one will get what [she] asks for. Every persistent seeker will discover what [she] longs for. And everyone who knocks persistently will one day find an open door. "Do you know of any parent who would give his hungry child, who asked for food, a plate of rocks instead? Or when asked for a piece of fish, what parent would offer his child a snake instead? If you, imperfect as you are, know how to lovingly take care of your children and give them what's best, how much more ready is your heavenly Father to give wonderful gifts to those who ask him?" - Matthew 7:7-11 MSG

Whether you're juggling classes, navigating new motherhood, or hustling in your career, remember: you can experience the beauty of attachment with God. It's never too late to experience His divine yeses and form a bond that brings wholeness and joy. Let's chat about this a little more. Sis, I really want to hear from your heart.

THE GIFT OF TRUST: MY PERSONAL JOURNEY

If you've ever felt disconnected or unsure about God, you're not alone. I grappled with my own faith against the backdrop of a complicated upbringing. I'm not pointing fingers; the adults in my life were navigating their own struggles and doing their best with what they knew, just like I am now. We're all imperfect, and none of us can fully embody the love and character of our good God. There are no perfect parents, except our Perfect Father, God. We all fall short of God's glory, and unfortunately, our loved ones are often on the receiving end of our imperfections and common struggle with sin.

Still, my environment as a young girl was tinged with neglect and emotional absence. Because of this, my understanding of God mirrored these flawed caregivers. He felt distant, cold, and, if I'm honest, kinda unreliable. But hey, it's pushed me on this transformative journey to break these generational chains and find God as He truly is—loving and reliable. Here's the turning point: I asked God, "Please reveal to me your goodness" and God gently whispered, "Put your trust in Me." He was inviting me to ask, to seek, to knock—to actually expect Him to come through. He wanted me to experience His faithfulness, His goodness, His fatherly nature up close- all things I longed for as a little girl.

Hesitant but hopeful, I took that leap of faith. I began asking God for my heart's hidden desires—a soulmate, a tight-knit family, a cozy home. I didn't think I was on God's priority list for those things. He proved me wrong. Over the next five years, every single prayer got answered, each in an astonishing way. And through these answers to prayers God revealed Himself to me. His tender fatherly nature. His goodness. His presence. His investment in me and my trust for Him. And it changed everything.

This journey has been full of miracles, no doubt. It's not just about finding love and building a beautiful life, it's about God taking my complicated past and turning it into something more meaningful.

But the most incredible part? Knowing that I matter to God. That's given me a foundation of trust that's become the rock I stand on now. My past struggles? They don't set my identity. Instead, God's redemption of them is solid proof of His mighty power and unwavering faithfulness towards me, every step of the way. I can look back and see that nothing I went through in life was wasted with the Lord. While He never caused the bad things that happened, He did in fact redeem them for my good and for His glory. And for that I shout out a big ol' 'hallelujah'!

God didn't just answer my prayers so many years ago; He changed my life's narrative. He took a girl who felt unseen and made her realize her worth. He transformed my trust issues into a relationship with Him that now fills me with an indescribable joy and an enduring peace, no matter what life throws my way.
So let me tell you, if you've ever felt like your past is too messy for a

redo, think again. Because the best part is, if He can do it for me, He can do it for you. Your past doesn't have to be a life sentence; it can be the backdrop for a redemption story that's just waiting to unfold. So, to every young woman reading this, whatever season you're in—know that God wants to build that same foundation of trust with you. It's this trust that will guide you through the peaks and valleys of life, wrapped in the security and peace that only a strong attachment to our Heavenly Father can provide.

Are you ready to take that journey of trust? Because let me tell you, once you start walking this path, there's no going back—and you won't want to.

"

Never doubt God's mighty power to work in you and accomplish all this. He will achieve infinitely more than your greatest request, your most unbelievable dream, and exceed your wildest imagination! He will outdo them all! - Ephesians 3:20 TPT

CYCLE OF ATTACHMENT

I've got to level with you: the whole prosperity gospel thing? They've got it wrong, sis. God doesn't dish out blessings because we tithe this percent or that or because we muster up 'enough' faith. I mean, can you imagine God playing by those rules? I know we sometimes think God's blessings are tied to how "good" we are, like how much we tithe or how often we're in church. But seriously, God's not keeping score. He's just good—plain and simple. He loves to spoil us, just like a parent surprising their child with her favorite snack on a bad day.

Remember that comforting feeling when mom or dad would hug you tight? God's got that same nurturing energy, but on a grander scale. He gave us the ultimate gift—His Son—so we could feel His love every day. And let me tell you, He's not done. He's like that parent who keeps the surprises coming, filling our lives with little moments that remind us we're loved.

I know you've had days when you felt invisible, sis. We all have. That feeling of being utterly alone? Trust me, I've been there too. But it's on those hard days that God leans in even closer. He wants us to lean on Him, to rely on His love when we're at our lowest. He's not a one-and-done God; He's in it for the long haul.

Want more joy? More peace? A life that feels like it's worth living? Let's start trusting God like we've never trusted anyone before. It might take time—trust isn't built overnight. But can you imagine the legacy we'll leave? A legacy of faith, of trust, of real love. Not just for us, but for everyone who comes after us. It's way more valuable than any material thing we could ever hope for.

YOUR FATHER, GOD CRAVES CONNECTION WITH YOU

How are you doing, sis? We've covered so much ground. We've talked about our relationship with God, comparing it to the closeness and emotional connectedness that we perhaps wish we had with our parents. You've heard my heart, and maybe you've seen a bit of your own journey reflected back.

Here's the golden nugget: God wants to be as close to us as we are to each other. Closer, even. He's craving that deep connection, the kind that carries us through the highs and lows, the kind that feels like home. The kind of love that accepts us as we are and soothes the inner wounds of rejection that often cast a shadow over our earthly relationships. So what's holding us back? Let's dive into this love story with God, where we learn to trust Him just as much as we trust each other. We've got this, sister. God's already laying down the welcome mat; all we have to do is step in.

LET'S SPILL THE TEA, SIS!

Trusting God wholeheartedly is an essential part of the vibrant, fulfilling life you're meant to have. When we allow God into our hearts, tearing down the walls we've built, we form an unshakeable bond with Him—a bond that sustains, heals, and brings immeasurable joy.

Take some time to marinate on this. Grab your favorite journal, light a candle, put on some soulful music, and let's reflect. Here are five questions for you to ponder as you sit with the truths we've covered:

> **Where are you at with your trust in God?** Can you identify any walls you've put up that are keeping Him at arm's length?

> **Reflect on the "Divine Yeses" in your life.** When have you felt God say "yes" to your prayers, needs, or longings? How did those moments make you feel about your relationship with Him?

> **How does the idea of God as your 'good and perfect parent' resonate with you?** Do you find it easy or challenging to view God as a daddy figure, especially based on your own upbringing?

> **As a young woman navigating life, what are some specific ways you can open up to God more?** How can you intentionally build a stronger attachment with Him?

> **Considering your past experiences, what steps can you take to deepen your trust in God?** What specific areas of your life need a stronger sense of attachment to Him?

As you sit with these questions, don't rush. Take as much time as you need to reflect and be honest with yourself. Know that your journey towards forming a deep, intimate relationship with God is a beautiful one, full of twists and turns. But guess what, sis? He's walking every step of the way with you, and He can't wait to show you just how loved you truly are. Keep breaking down those walls and letting your Abba Father's love in!

14

WHEN OUR STORIES DISTORT OUR VIEW OF GOD

And Break Down Our Chairs

irl, we need to have a real talk about why some of us find it so hard to trust and create those healthy attachments with God. If that's not you, then amen, that's fantastic! But if you're reading this and you're struggling, I want you to be super kind to yourself right now. Understand that life has thrown some pretty heavy bags at you, turning you into someone who might be a little scared, a bit angry, and perhaps even wounded. Let's face it, we've all been through stuff—yes, even in the most godly and loving homes—that makes handing over control to an unseen God a challenging feat.

I don't have to tell you that life ain't a fairy tale. Am I right? It's messy, filled with broken people and, yes, sin. It's almost like a puzzle with missing pieces. So, it's only human for us to struggle with reconciling a good God when bad things just keep happening. But, that's why we need to actively seek out God's truth and let it transform us.

For those of you who have been through it—abuse, neglect, you name it—let me tell you, God has a VIP section in His heart just for you. When we come from backgrounds that have, in essence, hurt us, it wreaks havoc on our mental and emotional health. You can't just compartmentalize pain and shove it in some forgotten corner of your mind. No way, girl. When one area of our life gets hit, it's like a domino effect; everything else takes a hit too.

When we're brought up in environments that don't value us, naturally, our lens for viewing God gets distorted. We end up painting a picture of God that looks more like a demanding CEO than a loving Father. We start believing these damaging narratives as the ultimate truth just because that's all we know.

Look, it's not entirely our fault. Our experiences have made us skeptical and our assumptions, based on those experiences, often twist the real picture. But here's the kicker: these assumptions don't just mess up our view of God; they also distort our view of life and ourselves. The narratives we believe start to rob us of the Gospel's fullness and the peace and joy that could be ours.

Sometimes we are so caught up in our stories that we lose sight of God's story. Let me lay it down for you: the story you tell yourself may not be the actual truth. Sometimes, it's the enemy messing with our heads. You see, we tend to universalize our individual experiences, and suddenly they define everything for us—including God.

But here's the liberating news: Our experiences and our past don't have the final say on who God is. He's constant. He's good. And attaching to Him properly unlocks a whole new level of life that's full of hope, something that neither the religious world nor anything else can give us.

And on another note: let's throw off those church-imposed distortions, shall we? Satan loves nothing more than to sit right there in church, whispering lies through a fiery sermon or an unloving leader. Instead, let's get raw and real in seeking God for ourselves. After all, the Bible says, "You will seek me and find me when you seek me with all your heart" (Jeremiah 29:13 ESV). And sis, personally speaking, I've experienced this to be the darn good Gospel truth.

LEARNING TO TRUST IN A GOOD GOD

Can we really chat about this thing called trust, especially when it comes to our faith? I've realized that many of us who are wrestling with trusting God are like saved skeptics—almost a special kind of nihilist. Yep, I'm calling myself out too. It's not like we've sat down one day and logically concluded that God doesn't exist. Nah, it's way subtler than that. It's this lingering, emotional disbelief that God is good—at least, not when we needed Him most. He felt far away when we faced abuse, absent during our formative years, and painfully silent while we battled depression.

Sound familiar? That's the enemy for you. He's been scheming to hijack our hearts since we took our first breath. Seriously, it's like Satan had his own notepad and was ticking off all the reasons to feed into our "Why I Can't Trust God" list, whispering those doubts into our ears just like he did with Eve. Every heartache, every tear was a chance for him to slither in with his deceitful mantra: "You can't trust God." And like Eve, we ended up drifting further away from God, emotionally and spiritually locked behind walls we didn't even realize we had built.

This, honey, is what I call modern Christian atheism—this subtle, passive-aggressive refusal to trust God because we don't actually know how good He is. We might not say it out loud, but it's a real struggle in the depths of our soul. And let's be honest, sometimes it feels easier to just stick to surface-level faith that doesn't ask too much from us. But that's a lie; it actually takes so much more from us in the long run. Real faith, the kind that brings us closer to God, requires vulnerability, honesty, and courage. It demands us to confront and overcome our trust issues, and girl, that's not a walk in the park.

So let's not settle for anything less than an authentic relationship with God. It's high time we start digging deep into what's been holding us back, and really get to know the God who's been trying to reach us through it all. We owe it to ourselves, and He certainly deserves it. Let's keep this convo rolling, shall we?

OUR LEGACY OF TRUST ISSUES

You know what's comforting? Realizing that I'm not the only one caught up in this struggle against the enemy's lies. This war for our hearts? It's ancient. We've inherited a legacy of trust issues that goes back to the Garden of Eden, where Adam and Eve first chose their way over God's. When God warned them about eating from the tree of knowledge of good and evil, He wasn't messing around. Though they didn't experience physical death immediately, they did die in other, devastating ways—emotionally, mentally, and spiritually. And I get it; I've been there. I've often trusted God with my eternal destiny but failed to rely on Him for the challenges I face here and now, essentially living in a spiritual purgatory- on earth.

But as I've grown in my faith, I've confronted the hypocrisy of my own double-mindedness. The Bible is clear about the pitfalls of such an approach:

"...for the one who doubts is like a billowing surge of the sea that is blown about and tossed by the wind. For such a person ought not to think or expect that he will receive anything [at all] from the Lord, being a double-minded man, unstable and restless in all his ways [in everything he thinks, feels, or decides]." James 1:6-8 AMP

To live a Gospel-centered life, full of wholeness and contentment, we need to conquer our doubts and fully trust in God's love and goodness—both for our lives here and now, and for heaven that awaits us. We can't play both sides. Either we trust Christ for all of it—now and forever—or we're missing the whole point. If you find yourself at a crossroads between full trust and lingering doubt, I urge you to move unhesitatingly toward complete faith in God. Be real with Him. Be raw. Be furious if you need to be. After all, He died to have that level of intimacy with us. Dive deep into a relationship with God that's stripped of pretense and overflowing with sincerity. No holding back.

Maybe you've got this trust thing all figured out. But if you don't, understand that you're far from alone. So many Christians go through life only half-committed, and as a result, they miss out on the genuine peace and joy that come from total surrender. So take that leap of faith. Trust that God will catch you. Because I promise you, He will.

LET'S SPILL THE TEA, SIS!

> **God as a CEO vs. Loving Dad:** Okay girl, let's be real. If God were a character in your life movie, who would He be? The demanding boss who's never pleased, or the warm, loving parent? How does that compare to the loving Father vibe this chapter is all about?

> **Shady Church Moments:** Ever felt like even in church, something was just off? Like maybe that sermon or that one leader is messing with your view of who God really is? Spill the tea—what happened and how did you deal?

> **Reality Check on Lies:** We all have those little lies we tell ourselves, right? What's on your "fake news" list about God, yourself, or life? How's that holding you back from that one-on-one connection with God?

> **Trust Issues 101:** Do you have VIP sections in your life where you're like, "Okay God, you can come in," and others that are a no-go zone? What's up with that, and how can we make the VIP section an all-access pass?

> **Heart & Soul Search:** The Bible says, "You'll find me when you seek me with all your heart" Jeremiah 29:13 NIV. So, what's your version of a spiritual glow-up? How can you slide into that Bible verse like it's a DM full of hope and authenticity?

Feel free to sit with these questions. I strongly encourage you, sis, to pray and really seek out the Lord during these 'Spill the tea' sessions. These are prompts to help you go deeper with your heavenly Daddy and build that trust. In addition to talking with God, Journal your thoughts, sometimes writing it out helps you see things more clearly.

15

THE MASKS WE WEAR:

When Religion Gets in the Way of Knowing God

Have you ever felt like you're going through the religious motions but missing the heart of it all? If so, this chapter is for you, because I've been there, too. Let's start with a story.

My twin brother and I couldn't be more different. Picture us in high school: he's the life of the party, effortlessly blending into any social scene. Me? I'm more comfortable in smaller settings, often lost in my thoughts or busy with my Fellowship of Christian Athletes meetings or afterschool girls bible studies.

Now, my brother never quite bought into the religious lifestyle I embraced. To him, it seemed like a long list of "thou shall nots," restrictions that stole away life's joys. Back then, I used to pray earnestly for him, burdened by the fear that he might not find salvation. But let's fast-forward a bit. As life unfolded, I began to realize that my own approach to faith was less a loving relationship with God and more a safety net I had created to avoid life's complexities and fears. I was essentially living a half-life, one that was technically religious but emotionally and spiritually stunted. Sound familiar?

I can't help but think that many of us, at some point, have been caught in this trap of "performative faith." We follow the rituals, say the right things, but inside, we're grappling with a spiritual void not to mention a deep void in our soul. We're like the "whitewashed tombs" Jesus spoke of—beautiful on the outside but empty within.

66

"For you are like whitewashed tombs, which outwardly appear beautiful, but within are full of dead people's bones..." Matthew 23:27 NIV

This is the question we need to face: Are we experiencing the full, abundant life Jesus promised, or are we settling for a hollow, rule-based version of Christianity? Because if it's the latter, we're not just shortchanging ourselves; we're also poorly representing the Gospel to those around us who need it the most.

If any of this resonates with you, stick around. This chapter is about breaking free from the lifeless routines and rediscovering a faith that is not only vibrant but also deeply fulfilling and true.

WHAT DOES WORSHIPING GOD REALLY MEAN, LADIES?

My spiritual journey has had its fair share of ups and downs—I'm sure yours has too. I've gone from being that overly religious kid—oh, you know the type—to someone who's found an authentic relationship with God, far removed from checkboxes and rituals. And let me tell you, life on this side is a breath of fresh air. I even got my skeptical twin brother curious about what makes my relationship with God so different now.

We were sitting in this old dive bar, you know, the kind that has peanuts on the floor and a jukebox in the corner. And out of nowhere, he goes, "So, what's the deal with worshiping Christ? Do I have to learn tongues or something? Should I be feeling guilty about swearing the other day?" But you could hear it in his voice—what he was really asking was, "How do I earn God's love?"

And this what I told him, and I want to share it with you too: "Mack, you can't earn what's already yours. God's love? It's a gift. You don't have to jump through religious hoops to get it. Forget speaking in tongues, guilt-trips, and all those 'shoulds' and 'shouldn'ts.' If you ever feel like you're walking on eggshells in your relationship with God, take a step back. That's not Him talking. When you're on the right path with God, you're going to feel peace and rest, kinda like a kid feels safe and loved in the arms of their parent. Religion will tell you to do more and be more; Christ simply says, 'Come to me, and rest.'"

I've been in this faith game for a while, but for a good portion of it I was -say ten years of it- I was still dragging around the weight of religion, still feeling like I was never quite "enough." If that's you, it's time to reevaluate what you're worshiping. Let's take it back to basics: Love God, love others, and find your rest in Christ. And let's say goodbye to religious baggage, once and for all. It's time for all of us to experience the peace and joy that comes with truly knowing God.

Here's the tea, sis, and it's piping hot: You can't earn what's already yours. That's right, God's love is not a VIP club with an entrance fee. You don't need to know church lingo, or feel guilty for that slip of the tongue last week. If you find yourself stressed, anxious, or just plain fearful about your relationship with God, hit the pause but-ton. That's not God making you feel that way, sis. When you're vibing with the Lord, you'll feel this overwhelming sense of peace. Imagine that safe, warm, snuggly feeling you get in your fave oversized sweat-er—that's what it's like.

So, whether you're a young momma juggling three kids and a million to-dos, or you're a single lady navigating the dating scene (or avoiding it, no judgment here!), or even if you're a college girl trying to balance classes, work, and a social life, listen up: God is not about penciling another item onto your todo list or perfection. Forget all those rules and must-dos that religion loves to pile on us. Christ says, "Come as you are." Messy bun, yoga pants with a side of spilled yogurt? He's just happy you showed up!

Darling, my wish for you is to embrace the freedom and the love God offers, without the baggage. Ditch the religious checklists and let's dive deep into what a relationship with God really looks like. Because trust me, that's where our Gospel truth is found. And we could all use a little more of that- it's so good ya'll.

THE GOD OF THE OLD TESTAMENT

As we sat there, Mack continued to work through all the fear keeping him from really accepting the simplicity of Christ's way. "What about all the laws? Is it bad that I have a tattoo? That I eat pork? There are so many rules, I don't know where to start." And girl, I totally get it. We look at the Old Testament, and it's like we see a God who's the polar opposite of the loving, happy deity we want to believe in. Christianity today feels like it's lost its way, with so many denominations misunderstanding the compassionate teachings of Christ laid out in the Bible. But here's my heart-to-heart with you, ladies: We can't just pick apart Scripture with plain logic or listen to it like it's some list of do's and don'ts. As I like to say, we've got to spirit-read. We have to let our spirits engage with the Word just as we are engaged in a daily, hourly, minute by minute love-relationship with Christ- through prayer. It's about asking God to let His wisdom and truth wash over us, bypassing all our preconceived notions and human reasoning.

Like I was telling Mack, let's try to grasp the entire message of the Bible, okay? At a glance, the Old Testament might paint a God who seems to be against everything we consider pleasurable or good in this life. But hold on, here's the twist: The laws, the sacrifices, the rules—they weren't about pleasing God. Actually, the opposite. God Himself says He doesn't want our sacrifices or our empty rituals. Forget that Catholic school confirmation certificate or that theology degree you might be clinging to; if you're relying on those to find favor with God, you're missing the point.

The harsh realities presented in the Old Testament were actually there to show us how utterly we fall short of the glory of our great God. Those rules were laid out to demonstrate just how much we need a Savior, how much we need God. Whether you're the 'bad girl' who parties all night, or you're the 'good girl' ticking off every religious box, guess what? In the eyes of God, we're all on the same playing field.

This notion rattled the self-righteous folks back in the day, and it still does. Remember, Jesus wasn't crucified by outlaws; he was put to death by religious leaders who were shaken by His message that shattered their life's work. They couldn't stand the idea that they weren't better than anyone else.

CONTINUING THE CONVERSATION: THE REAL PURPOSE OF THE OLD TESTAMENT

Okay, so let's get into it. Why was the Old Testament even written? Why all these laws and sacrifices? Was it to keep God happy? Nuh-uh. He's actually on record saying He can't stand all that empty ritual stuff. What God wants is to be your rock, your foundation— that's the whole point the Old Testament was trying to make.

Here's the deal: All those rules were there to show us just how far off the mark we really are. No amount of perfectionism, no meticulously followed set of rules can make us worthy of standing before God. What it comes down to is that we need a Savior; we need God. And guess what? In His grand scheme, none of us are clean enough, good enough, or holy enough to earn that spot. It's all about His grace, babe. Even if you've only ever done one thing wrong in your entire life, that alone makes you as much in need of grace as anyone else. So why stress about earning God's love when it's already yours for the taking, through faith in Jesus Christ?

So go ahead, take a breather and let that sink in. You're loved as you are -through the blood of Jesus Christ- not as you think you should be. And isn't that the most freeing thing ever?

THE GOLDEN QUESTION AND THE TRAP OF RELIGION

Finally, Mack hit me with *the* golden question: "Why do people keep worshiping in this legalistic way if it's not what God wants?" I could see the genuine confusion in his eyes. "It's because they're deceived, Mack, plain and simple. They've bought into the lie that God's love is something to be earned, rather than a gift to be received."

"You mean it's that easy?" His eyes started to mist up, the realization hitting him like a ton of bricks. "So easy that it makes you want to serve Him even more, doesn't it?" I could see him nodding, his tears now freely flowing. "That's the whole point, Mack. When you understand that you're loved unconditionally, you're motivated by love, not obligation." After all, we love because He first loved us. (1 John 4:19).

A DISTORTED IMAGE OF GOD

It breaks my heart to see how religion often distorts our view of God. It's like we put Him in this little box that fits our comfort zone but limits our understanding of His grandeur. We often find ourselves unintentionally becoming self-appointed gatekeepers of His grace, as if we're whispering, 'Can we genuinely revel in the beauty and en-joy-ment of God's created world while still leading a life centered on the Gospel?' It's a notion that's almost laughable! But deep down, do we truly, wholeheartedly believe that we should savor every aspect of our Creator and the things which flow from Him?

In truth, we've inadvertently domesticated God, unknowingly stripping Him of His awe-inspiring magnificence. We've turned faith into a sterile, sanitized checklist, devoid of the raw, human emotions and interactions that we were designed to experience and enjoy because they are inherently good! The pulse of this issue reverberates in how we approach church -what we chalk up our faith experience to- for many, it's a sporadic attendance, a Christmas and Easter affair, where sermons barely scratch the surface of God's profound complexities and the sheer, unadulterated goodness that He embod-ies. It's truly disheartening to see that many who identify as 'Chris-tians' often miss out on the depth, the intimacy, and the profound joy of God's presence.

So, we're left wondering, why do so many remain disengaged, uninterested, seemingly untouched by the boundless majesty of our Creator? Perhaps it's the breakneck pace of modern life, the constant distractions that divert our attention from the sacred. Or perhaps it's a misconception, a regrettable misunderstanding of faith as a dry and lifeless checklist, instead of the dynamic and, dare I say, pro-foundly romantic, ever-evolving relationship it's intended to be.

DIVINE LONGING: THE HEARTFELT ROMANCE OF FAITH

In our quest for convenience, there's a risk of missing the profound depths of God's love, the vast wealth of His wisdom, and the breathtaking beauty of His creation. It's crucial to remember that faith isn't a mere task on our to-do list; it's an ongoing journey of the heart, an endless exploration of the divine that beckons us to embrace every facet of our Creator's character and the world He crafted for us – to passionately romance us and draw us ever closer to Himself, much like bouquets of flowers, chocolate kisses, and the tender embrace of God through His creation. It's a passionate wooing, meant to draw us closer to our Creator with an irresistible, heartfelt longing.

We cannot divorce the deeply romantic, emotional, and intensely 'felt' elements from God, in whose image we were fashioned to reflect these qualities throughout the tapestry of life, both in creation and in our intimate communion with our Creator, knitting together a profoundly intertwined and passionately affectionate bond with all of life, as God created it.

THE LIMITATIONS WE IMPOSE

Isn't it absurd how we've turned faith into a glorified to-do list? We're missing the point, and we've forgotten how to be awestruck by God's splendor. Faith should be an invitation to dive into the depths of God's love, but we're so caught up in maintaining our "good girl" image that we end up settling for a shallow relationship with the Divine. The reality? We're just as spiritually lost as someone seeking enlightenment through yoga or a pilgrimage.

Think about it. Why are we so hung up on earning God's love when He's offering it freely? We spend so much time wondering how to rise above our human limitations to reach God, not realizing that He's already met us halfway. The world around us is a feast laid out by God for our pleasure and enlightenment, from the beauty of nature to the relationships we hold dear. You'll discover more about God's character in a simple afternoon at the botanical gardens than you ever will by adhering to some legalistic fast.

The difference between religious piety and true faith boils down to one thing: relationship. It's not about the checkboxes; it's about a living, breathing relationship with God that starts the moment you accept yourself as His beloved daughter. He's not looking for perfection; He's looking for you—just as you are, where you are. The moment you grasp this, you'll find a freedom and depth in your spiritual life that no amount of rule-following could ever offer.

TIME TO DROP THE ACT, Y'ALL!

Lots of folks go chasing after religion to find that "thing" that the world can't give them—happiness, wholeness, peace, you name it. But get this: religion's often the very thing messing up their search. It's like a hamster wheel of "doing stuff" to feel close to God, but we're actually running in circles. Yep, it's one of Satan's best tricks to keep us missing out on the real deal Jesus offers.

Now let's get real for a sec. What's religion doing for us? Building us up or tearing us down? C'mon, deep down, we know the answer. We end up with low self-esteem, low-key resenting God, and feeling guilty as heck. But here's a mind-blower: God actually wants us to enjoy life—like, really enjoy it. Can we mention John 10:10, again? Jesus says He came so we can have life and have it to the full. How amazing is that?

GOD'S EVERYWHERE, Y'ALL

The key to falling head over heels for God, and finding that inner peace and joy, is simple: experience His goodness in the here and now. Lean into it. Enough with the doom and gloom; let's soak up God's awesomeness all around us. That's what everything's here for—to show off how amazing God is.

In my own walk with God, I've realized that when I deny myself the good stuff in life, I'm actually keeping God at arm's length. He's inviting us to be our true, unique selves, no shame attached.

So, if we wanna get real with God and find that happiness we're all after, let's stop putting life in these little boxes—good or bad, heaven or hell, right or wrong. Let's make God a part of it all, like the bedrock underneath everything we do, and aim to make Him proud in every single moment.

True Christianity isn't a laundry list of do's and don'ts; it's a lifestyle where Jesus is in the mix of our whole messy, beautiful lives. Our wins, our losses, our laughs, our tears—God wants to be there through it all, not just the "churchy" parts.

A FRESH LOOK AT FAITH

Just like my brother Mack, I've been confused by the church. Whether you're peeking in from the outside or you're knee-deep in church culture, it's easy to feel like Christianity wants to change you—like you have to give up pieces of yourself to fit in. Mack was so put off by this, he walked away from God altogether. Who wants to live constantly second-guessing every word and action? The good news: God doesn't want this for you either. In fact, living this way is a different kind of hell.

A FLIPPED COIN BUT STILL THE SAME DARN COIN

Those who've never been weighed down by religious expectations, like Mack, may actually have a fresher take on what Jesus is all about. Trust me, I envy that clear-headed view. But there's another side to this coin. Ignoring your spiritual needs leaves you running in circles, chasing happiness you'll never catch. My twin and I have seen life from both sides of the spiritual pendulum, and neither extreme is a happy place to be.

THE JESUS BRIDGE

Here's where Jesus comes in: He wants to free us from the torment on both ends. I've been stuck in a cycle of trying to earn God's love, while my brother's been missing the point that true freedom comes from a relationship with Christ. You see, Jesus didn't wipe out the law; He fulfilled it perfectly. He came to free us from the self-destructive cycle of sin. We're not just free to run wild; we're free to live a meaningful life connected to God.

In the end, it's all about balance. Stray too far one way, and you're bound by religious rules; stray the other, and you're a slave to the world's empty promises. The only stable ground is a relationship with Jesus—a connection that enriches us, completes us, and truly sets us free.

We've got to realize that God didn't just come to save us from the hellish afterlife. Rather, He came to save us from the hells we experience right here on earth—be it depression, anxiety, rape, starvation, loneliness, perfectionism, insecurity, self-hate, unhappiness, or want. These are all the result of living in a world saturated with sin, a world fundamentally at odds with God's life-giving ways. And just look at Christ's palpable anger towards the Pharisees and religious leaders. It tells us that He's especially committed to saving us from the life-draining effects of religion, striving, and legalism.

UNVEILING GOD'S TRUE NATURE AND OUR MISCONCEPTIONS

We often read Scripture at face value, but it's much deeper than that. When Jesus speaks of heaven and hell, they're not just physical locations; they're states of mind, spiritual states of being that we experience now. If we truly grasp this concept, we'll come to see God not merely as a spiritual guide but as the source of all our dreams, plans, wants, and needs. We've got to change our perception of what we think God wants to take away from us because, in reality, He only wants to give—just as He gave Himself on the cross.

It's profoundly sad, but true: some people aren't afraid of Satan; they're afraid of God. This isn't just ironic; it's a tragic misunderstanding. Such a belief often leads people, like it led my brother and me at one point, to think that serving God means we can't have fun, enjoy life, or be our true selves. But as I've come to seek God on my own terms, free from religious constraints, I've realized how much my brother and I—and perhaps much of the church—have been deceived. So, I'm on a mission to help women understand the true nature of God because His essence and His gospel offer so much more than what we've been led to believe.

JESUS IS FOR YOU!

Do you know the difference between our God and all the other nearly 5,000 gods being worshipped by humanity? Our God is the only one who came down to serve us, to love us, and to die for us. He's the only one who desires a deep, authentic relationship with us based on love, not works. In contrast, every other god of the world you have to work up to—and guess what? You never get there! In that authentic communion with God, all the striving falls away. You're not a servant trying to earn your keep; you're a daughter basking in the love of the ultimate Father. And that, my friend, is where real faith begins.

Before we can place our full trust in Jesus, a light bulb needs to go off in our minds: Jesus is for us. Contrary to what religion may have taught us, He didn't come to earth so that we could make sacrifices for Him. He came to sacrifice for us.

God wants to bridge the gap between the divine and the human, allowing us to experience His presence and the benefits of that presence every single day. He aims to bring a little slice of heaven down to earth for us, right here and now, with a full revelation to come later.

God's work in us is not to deprive or constrain us, but to build us up and set us free in ways we've never imagined. He wants to restore everything we lost at the Fall, beginning with our ability to connect deeply with Him through a loving relationship. A relationship with Christ forms the foundation for a beautiful life—and let me tell you, sweet friend, this I've personally found to be incredibly, overwhelmingly true!

LET'S SPILL THE TEA - AND THIS TIME IT'S PIPING HOT!

Alright, sis, without the fluff let's get down to it.

> **Is God a Friend or a Frenemy to You?:** Let's get honest: Do you feel like God is more like a supportive friend or someone who's always judging you? Does it ever feel like He's keeping you from what you desire most? Or do you sense that, deep down, God is actually for you?

> **Balancing the Two Faces of God:** Many of us struggle to reconcile the God of the Old Testament with the loving and forgiving God of the New Testament. Do you find it hard to wrap your head around these different aspects of God's character?

> **Jesus as the Giver, Not the Taker:** Have you heard the perspective that Christ came to give us back what was lost—our joy, our sense of self, our life's beauty? Many times we fear Christ just wants to take the goodness right out of life when we choose to follow him! But this is so far from the truth! He didn't come and die for you to take from you but to give you everything lost in the Fall and more! How does this make you feel? Does it make you more inclined to lay your life down before our perfect and loving Christ?

> **Are You in a Spiritual Limbo?:** Sometimes we find ourselves stuck in a spiritual in-between. Do you want a relationship with God but are hesitant to fully trust Him? What's holding you back? What do you need from God to get there? It's okay, sis. Be honest with God and tell him!

> **Your Slice of Heaven on Earth:** Yes, heaven and hell are physical places. Scripture is very clear on that. But have you considered that heaven and hell could also be states of being right

here, right now? What are some ways you can experience a bit of 'heaven on earth' through your faith?

> **The Foundation of it All:** Your Relationship with Christ: We can talk all day about spirituality, but at the end of the day, have you accepted Christ as your savior? Because the truth is, nothing we discuss will truly resonate without that foundation. If you haven't, is today the day you're willing to take that step? If so, girl, I'm PRAISING Jesus! Skim below and let's chat some more.

THE GOSPEL GOOD NEWS

Next Step: Inviting Jesus In

Hey there, sweet sis. One of my favorite verses of all time is John 3:16. This is the Gospel in a nutshell: "For God so loved the world that He gave His one and only Son, that whoever believes in Him shall be saved." The Bible is clear: "If you declare with your mouth, 'Jesus is Lord,' and believe in your heart that God raised Him from the dead, you will be saved" (Romans 10:9 NIV). So are you ready, girl? Are you ready to invite Jesus into your heart and put that foundation underneath your chair? If so, say this prayer with me but remember it's not about saying some words. It's about the heart. A heart that wants Jesus.

Dear Lord Jesus,

I know that I am a sinner, and I ask for Your forgiveness. I believe You died for my sins and rose from the dead. I turn from my sins and invite You to come into my heart and life. I want to trust and follow You as my Lord and Savior. I know I won't do this perfectly; I live in a broken world, and I know this prayer doesn't make me perfect but it covers my imperfections with your blood sacrifice that you made for me. So I ask you to come into my heart and be the change in me, Jesus. Through the highs and lows of my life, walk beside me. And carry me when I'm too weak to do it alone. Be my all in all, Jesus. Amen.

Ahhhhhmennn! Can you hear me screaming at the top of my lungs and praising Jesus for you! I'm proud of you, sis. This is just the start. Life is so good when connected to our Creator, and our life source! Just a note though, while Jesus is constantly working and molding us more into His image throughout our lives after salvation, through a process called sanctification, salvation itself is a momentary decision. You did not earn it, and you cannot lose it, no matter what you do or fail to do. "For it is by grace you have been saved, through faith—and this is not from yourselves, it is the gift of God" (Ephesians 2:8 NIV). Hallelujah for that, amen, sis?

So go on, sis. Go and tell someone the life-changing decision you just made! And welcome to the family of God!

Part 5:

WHEN YOU'RE READY FOR
DEEP SIPS AND SOUL TALKS

16

JESUS & COFFEE

❝

Busyness is an illness of the spirit. - *Eugene Peterson*

As dawn breaks, I find myself sitting on my porch, coffee in hand, whispering prayers while the sun rises over the tree line. My mornings have become much simpler these days. Gone are the chaotic early hours where I'd whirl around, ambitiously praying and ticking off a meticulously organized list of petitions to the Lord. Fear had taken the driver's seat in my relationship with God, leaving little room for Him to actually speak back to me.

You see, I used to conduct my quiet times like a business meeting with God, like He was a secretary taking down my demands. I'd follow prayer guidelines, create prayer maps, and thought I was making God my priority, but I was missing the point. The "to-do" lists, the sacrifices, the control—they were all distractions. God met me even in my flawed approach, thank God for that. But recently, He's been urging me to make room for something more—stillness.

Unhurried and unguarded, I've begun to speak to God like

one would converse with a friend. No agendas, no bullet points, just heart-to-heart talks about what really matters—my hopes, my fears, even my neighbor in need next door. And it's uncomfortable, to be honest. As someone who has always avoided diving into her own feelings, I find it challenging. But God "does feelings," and I can't fully connect with Him unless I'm willing to be vulnerable with both Him and myself.

I'm also learning to listen—really listen. It's in the moments of awkward silence that God moves. His voice may not be audible, but His Spirit works in mysterious ways, guiding my thoughts and pulling my heart towards Him. The less I strive, the more time I have to still my heart before Him, and that, I'm discovering, is all He truly wants.

I've relinquished the routines, the habits, and the legalistic readings of Scripture that I once believed would bring me closer to God. I've found freedom in sitting at Jesus' feet like Mary—simple, humble, and open. Along the way, I've met a different God from the one I was taught about, and it's been eye-opening. Because in the end, the Kingdom of God isn't something to be dissected by theologians; it's to be received like a child, free from complexity and pretension.

Jesus tells us in Luke 18:15-17 that whoever does not receive the kingdom of God like a little child will never enter it. I used to think deeper theological studies would bring me closer to God, but all they did was create distance, filling my mind with doubt and fear. Now I understand that simple faith and authentic closeness to the Lord offer wisdom and discernment beyond what any theology degree or sermon can provide.

My spiritual journey began, and will end, on this porch with just Jesus and coffee, because at its core, it's all about that simple, profound connection. I've found that this new way of living—of just being present—has also improved my overall mindfulness. It's a healing pace, a life less focused on tomorrow and more invested in today.

While the world rushes by, I'm okay with being left behind in this quiet moment, away from the chaos and the relentless quest for "more." And while I might daydream about a secluded home out West or a cute beachside retreat, for now, I'm content to be exactly where I am—on this quiet porch, with Jesus and coffee. Here, with Jesus and my coffee, I find what truly matters: a simple, heartfelt connection with God. And isn't it beautiful, how uncomplicated it all really is?

LET'S SPILL THE TEA, SIS!

Oh hey howdy hey, lovely souls! It's time for some serious heart-to-heart. If you've got your coffee and your fave cozy blanket, then you're all set for today's convo, which comes straight from my own journey of spiritual growth. You see, when I allowed God into every nook and cranny of my heart—dreams, fears, and everything in between—something extraordinary happened. It felt like a soothing balm on all my uncertainties, like a reassuring hand telling me, "I got you."He showed me just how deeply He cares, how much He wants to be a part of every detail in my life, and how much He's willing to invest in me. He's also revealed to me what a Dream Giver our God is!

He's revealed a deeply personal side to our relationship that allows me to dream big, to desire, and to receive His blessings. And guess what? All of this transformation has happened during my precious "Jesus and coffee" moments. I'm telling you, those moments are sacred. So, today's "spill the tea" session is going to be a bit longer than usual, but trust me, this is where the real magic happens, sis!

> **Morning Routines:** What does your morning routine currently look like? Is there room to fit in a coffee date with Jesus?

> **Self-Care vs. Soul Care:** How do you balance self-care rituals like skincare or workouts with soul care moments like spending time with God? What are some things you'd like to include in your daily and weekly soul care routine?

> **Busy or Productive:** Are you busy or are you productive?

How is your constant busyness affecting your spiritual life and your peace of mind? Are there things you can gracefully bow out of to make more space for soul care?

> **God as a Friend:** How would you feel texting God like you text your BFF? Do you think you can be that casual and honest in your prayers?

> **Dreaming with God:** What are some of your deepest heart's desires that you can begin to bring before Him during your "Jesus and coffee" time? Psalms 37:4 says, "Delight yourself in the Lord, and he will give you the desires of your heart." Can you relate any personal experiences to this? How can you begin dreaming with God? (Hint: consistency and persistence has always proven to be the key for me (Luke 11:5-13)).

> **#NoFilter with God:** How can you be more 'unfiltered' in your conversations with God? Is there something you've been holding back from saying to Him? He's a big God, he can handle it. And he wants it, because at the end of the day he wants YOU- even the hard parts, because he'll be the one to soften them!

> **Awkward Silences:** How do you deal with awkward silences in your daily life? Could embracing these moments help you hear God more clearly?

> **Your Emotional Baggage:** What emotional baggage are you carrying that you find difficult to discuss, even with God?

> **Insta-worthy or Real:** How often do you seek "Insta-worthy" spiritual experiences over authentic connection with God?

> **Fear of Missing Out:** Do you ever feel FOMO for worldly experiences when you choose to spend time with God? How do you deal with this feeling?

> **Simple Pleasures:** What are some simple pleasures that bring you joy and could be seen as gifts from God?

> **Your Dream Life:** If you could create a highlight reel of your dream life, what would be on it? How does your faith fit into this vision? Could this bring you closer to God and bring Him glory? What would it look like for you to invite God in to these dreams and to partner with God to make them a reality?

> **Social Media vs. Scripture:** How does the time you spend scrolling through social media compare with time spent reading scripture or praying? Is there room for balance?

17

THE GOSPEL TABLE:

Pull Up A Seat, Sis!

et's be real, ladies. The struggle is so real when it comes to balancing our roles as moms, wives, students, or simply fabulous single women. Add to that our struggle to break through surface-level relationships, and you've got a one-way ticket to Loneliness Town. I get it; I've been there too. As someone who's always been a social chameleon—able to switch from "mom mode" to "work mode" effortlessly—I still found myself shying away from meaningful, soulful interactions. I had my squad, yes, but not the kind of friendships where I could bare my soul without a second thought.

But God has been speaking to my heart, sister-friends. And He's saying, "Enough with the fluff! Go deep!" Over the past year, I've felt the Lord urging me to go beyond casual friendships and step into authentic community. And you know what? That's where the magic happens. That's where we find not only friendship but also spiritual sisterhood, genuine joy, and—yes, I'm going to say it—wholeness.

What does it look like to 'go deep,' you ask? Picture this, sis: I started inviting couples into my home, not for picture-perfect dinner parties but for soul-satisfying gatherings. We break bread, spill tea about our lives, and have those raw, unfiltered conversations that women of God crave but seldom find space for. And, wow, has it been freeing! The transparency, the intimacy—it's refreshing for the soul and healing for the heart.

So why am I sharing this with you, especially in one of our final chapters about finding beauty and wholeness in Christ? Because, my dear sisters, we can't do it alone. True happiness, real peace, and soul-deep wholeness come to life when we're in authentic community. It's how God designed us. We're wired to belong, to share, and to live life together.

You know, Jesus was all about community, too. He could have gone about His ministry alone, but He chose to gather disciples, share meals, and create spaces for real talk. Jesus shows us that community isn't a "nice-to-have"; it's a "must-have" for living a Christ-centered life.

COMMUNITY AS A PATH TO WHOLENESS

Let's take a leaf out of His book, shall we? As we wrap up this spiritual journey, I invite you to take your seat at the Gospel Table, where there's always room for one more. Let's drop the act, toss aside our to-do lists for just a moment, and focus on what really matters: connecting on a deeper level with each other and with God.

So as you go about your day—whether you're juggling carpool duty, tackling another college essay, managing household chaos, or simply searching for your place in this world—remember that you're never alone. The table is set, and your sisters in Christ are waiting for you. It's time to sit down, dig in, and taste the wholeness

God has prepared for each of us.

And that, lovelies, is how we find our way back to ourselves, back to each other, and most importantly, back to the heart of God. So here's to community, to vulnerability, and to living life authentically. Cheers, sisters!

REDEFINING CHURCH: MORE THAN BRICKS, BEYOND SUNDAYS

What if connections with our God Gals aren't meant to be found solely in the hustle and bustle of church buildings and Sunday services? It's a thought-provoker, isn't it? When it comes to finding our community rooted in Christ, we often default to the idea that it's all about the church building. But let's hit the pause button and redefine what "the church" actually is. According to Scripture, the church isn't a pile of bricks and stained glass; it's two or more believers—yes, just a duo—whose hearts are set on Jesus. So in essence, the church is you and me in a room, totally focused on our Savior. So really, we can bring the church anywhere because we **are** the church.

BEYOND THE PEWS: REDISCOVERING JESUS' VISION FOR AUTHENTIC COMMUNITY

Now, let's keep it 100, girl. Our contemporary way of "doing church" can sometimes feel as unfulfilling as a candy bar for breakfast. Quick to grab, but oh-so lacking in what truly nourishes us. It's like we're all running on a churchy treadmill, busy but not fulfilled. The gospel table that Jesus modeled was about more than just a pit stop on Sundays. It was about gathering in homes, around campfires, or at tables, sharing meals, stories, and prayers—the authentic Acts church in action.

TABLE TALKS: JESUS-STYLE COMMUNITY IN A MODERN WORLD

Somewhere along the way, we've missed the mark. The art of true connection and disciple-making has gotten lost in the fray. Instead of meaningful connections that radically transform lives, we're often left with shallow interactions limited to the church building. It's time to return to the authentic community Jesus modeled, one centered not just around a building, but around the body of believers in genuine, life-giving fellowship.

If we could travel back to when Jesus was walking the Earth, we'd find a very different model for church. He spent time with his disciples in simple settings—around tables, breaking bread. The church that Jesus modeled was intimate, authentic, and deeply personal.

The reality I've found, personally, is that I simply cannot get this intimate Jesus-centered experience at church. It's too big. Too distracting from the basic elements necessary to really build an authentic soul to soul connection with Jesus and others.

As you slow down and truly connect, you'll find that something incredible happens. Sharing meals with people around my table has become soul food in more ways than one. It's not just about nourishing our bodies; it's about nourishing our souls and our spirits, too. This gathering allows us all to hit the pause button on life's craziness and focus on what really matters: deep, fulfilling relationships. Believe me, sharing a meal with someone is as intimate as it gets without crossing into physical territory. It's a sacred space, free from the usual distractions and overstimulation that so often makes social interactions feel superficial. Instead, what we're left with is an unfiltered, soul-to-soul connection that dares us to dig deep. I love this. I think Jesus loves this too.

This kind of intentional gathering creates a space where we can share the Gospel and foster gospel-centered conversations. It allows us the freedom to be vulnerable and speak soul truths. It lets us lead each other and disciple each other in life-giving ways. Whether you're a mom, student, wife, or happily single, this form of "church" allows for the kind of authentic connections that Jesus Himself modeled.

God has recently given me a vision for how to "do church" that's much closer to home. Instead of rushing off to a mega-church every Sunday, I'm inviting people into my own living space. And before I step on any toes, can I be super honest? My years of serving in a large church community have often felt disconnected from both God and those I was trying to minister to. In contrast, gathering around a table helps us get back to the basics of what church and community should be—a fellowship that brings us closer to God and each other in the most beautiful, intimate ways.

Sis, let's go back to the roots of our faith, following Jesus' model of intimate, personal connection. It's time to make space for church that not only fills our bellies but also nourishes our souls. It's about time we embrace this model for doing church, don't you think?

THE TABLE: OUR 'SHABBAT SHALOM'

Alrighty, you gorgeous souls! Are y'all ready to unpack the ultimate life hack straight from the Bible? Yep, we're diving into 'Shabbat Shalom,' and no, it's not a trendy skincare routine or the name of a new yoga pose. It's like a VIP invitation to a weekly soirée hosted by none other than God Himself.

So, let's break it down. Shabbat is Hebrew for rest, and Shalom is all about peace, wholeness, and that inner glow that no makeup can replicate. Combine them, and it's like God's personalized care package for our lives, delivered every weekend from Friday night to Saturday evening. And, get this—it includes three lavish meals, aka 'seudos,' to share with your tribe. Food, family, and faith—sounds like a heavenly trifecta to me!

Now, I know we're programmed to think of Sabbath as a series of 'Thou Shalt Nots.' But hear me out, loves, that's old-school thinking! The Sabbath isn't some divine limitation; it's our spiritual playground. Imagine a day carved out by God, where the to-do list includes feasting, relaxing, and soul-level convos with our nearest and dearest.

THE DIVINE POETRY OF TASTE: FINDING GOD IN EVERY FLAVOR AND GATHERING

Ya'll, did you know that we have over 10,000 taste buds?! I can't help but think that food is more than just sustenance.[8] Food isn't just fuel for our bodies; it's like God's own poetry, a creative masterpiece meant to engage our senses and enrich our souls. Think about it— over 10,000 taste buds are not an accident or even a coincidence. They're a design feature, an intentional brushstroke of love from the Ultimate Artist. Every bite, every flavor, is a way of God saying, "Hey, I adore you, and I've made this world deliciously beautiful for you to experience." It's more than nourishment; it's a moment of grace, an embrace of love, and a true work of art. I mean, can we get an "Amen"? That's not just biology; that's Divine RSVP to savor life in all its fullness!

THE SACRED TABLE: WHERE NOURISHMENT MEETS SOUL AND 'SHABBAT SHALOM' COMES TO LIFE

Here's the 411: the table isn't just a piece of furniture; it's more like a sanctuary that serves up hefty portions of nourishment for the body, soul, and spirit. Think about it: a space where we can laugh, share, eat, and pray? That's not just socializing, darlings; that's 'Shabbat Shalom' in action. To put a cherry on top, let's sprinkle in a little ancient wisdom with a traditional Hebrew prayer: "Blessed are you, O Lord God, King of the Universe, for you give us food to sustain our lives and make our hearts glad." That's not just a prayer, sis; that's a whole mood!

THE TABLE: WHERE HEARTS CONNECT

All right, we've been diving deep into this idea that the table is more than just a piece of furniture—it's a space for all things peace and nourishment. But hold on a sec, let's unpack that a bit more. What about moving beyond the food and diving into soul-level connections?

Imagine this: the table as your personal heart-and-soul oasis. This is where we get to put down our phones and pick up meaningful connections. It's where we move from small talk to soul talk, all while passing the mashed potatoes. And let's not underestimate the power of friendship and connection. Psychologists are always raving about how strong social connections contribute to our mental and even physical well-being. They're like the avocado to your toast— absolutely essential!

HEART-TO-HEARTS AROUND THE TABLE: A PACT FOR AUTHENTIC FRIENDSHIPS AND SOULFUL CONNECTIONS

Y'all, we're missing out big time if we don't embrace the sheer magic of gathering around the table. In a world where we're always hustling and glued to our screens, what our hearts are really aching for is a long, soul-filling meal with our tribe—quality time and heart-to-hearts with our inner circle, right around the dinner table!

Okay, let that sink in. In a world that's running on 5G, sometimes we need to take it down to 1G—a single gathering, with real faces and real grace. Friendships are life's seasoning, adding flavor and texture to our daily grind. Genuine friendships give us that safe space to be ourselves, to 'spill the tea' about our lives, and to walk away feeling seen and heard. Trust me, it's more refreshing than any detox tea out there.So, can we make a pact? Let's promise to invest in those real, authentic friendships that make our souls sing. It starts by inviting them to your table, both literally and figuratively. And watch how these connections blossom into the most beautiful bouquets in the garden of life.

THE TABLE: WHERE THE 'UNLOVABLE' MEET GRACE AND SIN FINDS A SEAT

You know how everyone always says, "Come to church, feel the love, find your tribe"? But what if I told you that Jesus Himself laid down a different kind of red carpet for those looking for love and acceptance? Yes, darling, Jesus was the ultimate host, but not just at any venue—He chose the dinner table. Now, let me spill some divine tea. Jesus wasn't just munching on loaves and fishes with His disciples. Nope, He was setting the table for the 'unlovables,' the overlooked, and yes, the sinners. The table was His ministry, His pulpit, and His stage.

Think about it, girl. Through His example of ministry in the Gospels, Jesus is teaching us that true outreach isn't limited to a church building with a steeple. The real power move is inviting people to your table—yes, your IKEA dining set or that cute little breakfast nook. When we break bread together, it's like we're breaking down walls, too. And let me tell you, there's no sermon more impactful than the unspoken love shown through shared spaghetti or a communal pot of chili.

Can we pause and marinate on some truth for a moment? This is Jesus' heart laid out for us, ya'll:

"And as Jesus reclined at the table in the house, behold, many tax collectors and sinners came and were reclining with Jesus and his disciples. And when the Pharisees saw this, they said to his disciples, 'Why does your teacher eat with tax collectors and sinners?' But when he heard it, he said, 'Those who are well have no need of a physician, but those who are sick. Go and learn what this means: "I desire mercy, not sacrifice." For I came not to call the righteous, but sinners.'" Matthew 9:10-13 ESV

I mean, let's talk about it. Who's really showing up at church on a Sunday morning? It's generally people who are already believers, right? The very ones Jesus says don't need a "physician." We get so preoccupied with church programs, worship setlists, and fancy lattes in the café that we forget about those who are truly hurting and in need of God's mercy. Girl, Jesus is serving us some serious truth tea! We often get stuck in this loop of

Sunday morning rituals, right? But Jesus is like, "Hold up. The people who really need you aren't even in the building."

Jesus was chilling with tax collectors and sinners—folks who wouldn't step foot in our modern-day churches. He wasn't just sitting in the synagogue waiting for people to come to Him. Nah, He was out there in the streets, in homes, sharing meals, and having real conversations. So why are we confining ourselves to church walls when the people who need us most are out there?

Now, let's dish about 'mercy.' It's not just a word; it's an embrace. To show mercy means to tenderly embrace the unlovable, the ones we might instinctively turn away from. Picture it: arms wide open, heart full of God's love, reaching out to someone who's been rejected or pushed to the sidelines. That's the Jesus-style hug we're aiming for.

By inviting people to our tables, we're not just saying, "Hey, here's a meal," we're saying, "Hey, here's a safe space to be you." It's about letting people know they're seen, valued, and loved just as they are—flaws and all. And honestly, isn't that what the Gospel is about? Creating spaces of love and acceptance where religious tracts and formal invites have failed.

What if our next outreach isn't a church event but a simple dinner invitation? Imagine the kind of soul-touching, life-changing convos that can happen between the 'pass the salt' and the last sip of sweet tea. That's doing it Jesus-style, and trust me ya'll, it's a vibe He wants us all to catch. Let's not just save seats in our sanctuaries; let's set places at our tables. Because according to Jesus, that's where the real ministry happens. Amen? Amen.

So go ahead, shake up your guest list! Invite the friend who's struggling, the neighbor who's different, and the family member who's difficult. When we open our homes and hearts, we also open the floodgates for God's grace to flow, showing everyone that they, too, are welcome in His Kingdom.

Oh, girl, let's get down to the real, soul-stirring truth as we wrap up this chapter. What if the whole idea of "doing church" could be as cozy and intimate as having your closest friends around your dining table? You know, the way Jesus did it. He wasn't in megachurches; He was breaking bread in people's homes making soul-level connections. That's where the real ministry happened, sis, and I'm starting to see why.

THE UNSCRIPTED CHURCH AT MY KITCHEN TABLE

Our hearts crave deep, genuine friendships in the same way our bodies crave nourishment. I don't think that's a coincidence; I think that's God's divine design. The table isn't just a place to eat; it's a place to fill our souls and connect on a level that's more than skin-deep.

Now, get this. I've been hosting monthly game nights with my soul sisters from the life group that my hubby and I attend. We've been doing Bible studies too, and let me tell you, it's been a spiritual game-changer. I've gone beyond surface-level relationships and started investing in connections that really dig deep.

Our Tuesday Life Group sessions are enriching, don't get me wrong. But when it's just a few of us, gathered around delicious homemade food, that's when the walls come down. That's when we swap small talk for big truths, and let me tell you, it feels like a holy moment every single time. And as I shut off my porch light at the end of the night, I can't help but feel this profound sense of fulfillment. It's as if my cup isn't just full; it's overflowing. We often think church has to be this grand affair with a strict schedule and designated roles. But what if it could be as simple, and as profound, as sharing a heartfelt meal and diving into the Word together?

FINDING MY SOUL'S TRUE JOY IN REAL, JESUS-CENTERED CONNECTIONS

Y'all, I am living for this new approach to faith and friendship. It's grounded me, filled me with a sense of peace—shalom, if you will—and above all, it's made me incredibly happy.

I've even taken a break from the constant scrolling on social media. Instead, I'm diving into prayer and practicing mindfulness. Because at the end of the day, I want a life that's rich in love, both for myself and for others. And honestly, no amount of likes or follows can compare to the deep joy of real, Jesus-centered community.

So, I've recently said goodbye to my social apps and taken to prayer and deep breaths instead; you know, when I want something to scroll, something to distract, something to excite. I'm no longer connecting artificially on social media platforms, rigid church routines, and unintentional relationships. Because at the end of the day I want to love my life and I want to love others well too— and I can't honestly say that my lifetime spent in a church building has aided me in either of these two things very effectively, if that's what I chalk my spiritual life up to. All the ways I try to connect around busyness and noise and service can never replace the simple way Jesus modeled for us: dining around the gospel table.

So, here's the deal. I've found what fills my soul, and it's not pews or pulpits or Instagram feeds. It's the people around my table, the laughter in the air, the Bible opened before us, and the presence of God all around. And let me tell you, sis, it's everything.

LET'S SPILL THE TEA, SIS!

Okay, sis, take a breath—that was a lot of goodies packed into one nourishing protein bar, am I right? Our "spill the tea" session is getting real, and we're diving into the good stuff we often gloss over. I want to chat with YOU, sis! I'm eager to hear your thoughts and feelings on everything we've just unpacked. So for this "spill the tea" session, we're doing things a bit differently. I've broken it all down and filtered out the fluff, so we can focus on the real gems. Take your time to move through these! This session isn't meant to be sipped down all at once. Instead, go at your own pace. We can chat a little or as much as you want. You set the pace! These self reflection questions are here for YOU! No pressure, okay? With that being said, let's unpack these questions to truly digest what we've learned and go live out our Gospel- beautifully!

FIRST UP? RELATIONSHIP DEPTH:

> **Friendship Filter:** Are your friendships more about playdates and Pinterest-worthy gatherings than meaningful conversations? Where's the depth missing?

> **Squad Goals:** You have your brunch buddies, but do you have soul sisters for late-night talks? What keeps you from diving deep?

AUTHENTIC COMMUNITY:

> **The Real Deal:** You know that instant comfort of being yourself—what's your version of an authentic community, and how can you make it happen?

> **Sunday Scenarios:** Is your church experience a spiritual 'quick fix,' or is it more like a nourishing soul-feast?

FAITH JOURNEY:

> **Going Jesus-Style:** What if you channeled your inner Jesus and opted for intimate, heartfelt dinners? How could this transform your faith journey?

> **Home Truths:** Got cold feet about opening your home for genuine gatherings? What fears hold you back and how can you kick 'em to the curb?

INCORPORATING 'SHABBAT SHALOM':

> **Weekend Vibes:** How can you weave 'Shabbat Shalom' into your hectic lifestyle? Got any ideas to make it a family or friends affair?

> **Tradition Twist:** Did you know the original Sabbath was like an all-day self-care ritual? How does this compare to your usual Sunday service?

RETHINKING SABBATH AND SERVICE:

> **Flip the Script:** How about flipping Sabbath to Friday evening to Saturday, then making Sunday your 'give-back' day? Could this 'fill and pour' approach be your new spiritual game-changer?

QUESTIONS ABOUT THE TABLE: WHERE HEARTS CONNECT:

> **Heart-to-Hearts, Anywhere:** When was the last time you

went beyond small talk, whether that's at the dining hall table or the family dinner table? What sparked that conversation?

> **Who's in Your Tribe?:** From study buddies to mom friends, who are the people you want to deepen your connections with? How can you make it happen this month?

> **Time-Stealers:** What's stealing your 'connection time'? Is it schoolwork, toddler tantrums, or maybe work deadlines? How can you mix in time for connection amidst the chaos?

> **From Functional to Family:** Whether it's a dorm room desk or your kitchen island, how can you transform your 'functional space' into a 'family space' to connect intentionally?

QUESTIONS ABOUT THE DINNER TABLE: WHERE THE 'UNLOVABLE' MEET GRACE AND SIN FINDS A SEAT

> **Dining with Divinity:** How do you feel about Jesus choosing the dinner table as His ministry platform? Does that shake up any of your preconceptions?

> **The Uninvited:** Who in your life—be it on campus or in your community—feels overlooked or less loved that you could invite in? What's holding you back?

> **Spreading the Good News at Supper:** Whether it's turning your dorm room into a communal eatery or your dining room into a haven, how can you use what you've got to prepare a meal and share the Gospel goodness?

QUESTIONS ABOUT SOCIAL MEDIA AND REAL CONNECTION:

> **Scroll or Soul?:** How does your screen time compare to your soul time? Are you spending more moments scrolling or connecting?

> **Digital Detox Dare:** Whether you're a busy mom or a stressed student, have you considered a break from social media? What's stopping you?

> **IRL Goals:** What real-life steps can you take this week to move from screen-time buddies to real-time friendships?

18

GOSPEL HUNGRY CHURCH

Brené Brown describes our era as "the most medicated, addicted, overweight cohort of history,"[9] and that line never leaves me. It's a wakeup call that something's broken—in our lives and perhaps in our churches too. Modern life piles on the stress, and what's meant to be our spiritual refuge sometimes adds to the burden.

I've gotta be honest: for too long, I've confused my dedication to Christ with my commitment to a church building. I've felt drained, constantly being asked to serve more, fill in the gaps, and extend myself until I had nothing left to give. And the sad part? I felt that the more I served, the more disconnected I became.

As a faithful member of my local church, I've been like Martha in the kitchen who was busy cooking, serving, and planning while missing the Jesus experience happening in the living room. If she'd just put a stop to her tasks and joined the others sitting at His feet, she'd have caught the moment. Similarly, I've missed Jesus' presence and the presence of my fellow Christians that happens when I stop my busyness for the Lord. He really doesn't need it, and I see throughout Scripture that He doesn't want it either.

Sunday mornings became another checkbox on my to-do list. Instead of coming back recharged, I left feeling just as stressed, anxious, and empty as before. This is the spiritual wholeness Brené Brown talks about missing in modern life, and it's certainly what I thought religion would bring me- but it never did.. So, let's get real here. I've rarely felt a deep, soulful connection at the church building. It's more like a social hub than a spiritual home. If this keeps up, the church body is in for a wake-up call, y'all!.

Maybe it's time to redefine church—not as a place we go, but as a community where we genuinely engage with God and each other. Because, really, if we're as "hungry" as Brené Brown suggests, isn't it time we found the right kind of nourishment?

IF YOU WANT TO KNOW JESUS, COME TO CHURCH...OR MAYBE DON'T?

Listen up. For years, I thought the key to my spiritual journey was tied to those Sunday sermons, stained glass windows, and hymnals. We've all heard it, right? "The church is where you meet Jesus, where your faith takes shape, and transformations happen." But let me spill some real tea: that's not the complete story. Now, don't get me twisted; my local church is a blessing y'all. But when you strip it down, it's just a building—four walls, some steeples, maybe a cross, and rows of pews. What brings that place to life? It's the spirit we walk in with and whether we allow Jesus to have the spotlight.

The Good Book even tells us that church can happen wherever we make room for it. Jesus laid it out: "For where two or three gather in my name, there am I with them" (Matthew 18:20, NIV). So, want to live that real-deal #JesusLife? Look no further than your own home, babe. It's at the dinner table, during those bedtime prayers, and in those day-to-day lessons we show our kids—or anyone else in our circle—through how we act and what we do. And let's not forget, it's also in what we intentionally choose to talk about. The topics we lean into can be mini sermons in themselves, showing what really matters to us. Remember, 'out of the mouth the heart speaks.' So, what's consuming your conversations lately?

FROM CHURCH WALLS TO HEART HALLS: REALIGNING OUR SPIRITUAL PRIORITIES AND LIKEWISE OUR COMMUNITY

Here's where it gets personal: I realized that my attachment to the church building was siphoning off precious time I could be using to genuinely connect with God's people—starting with my own fam. To live that fulfilling spiritual life Jesus talks about, I had to do some soul-checking and draw some boundaries. First stop? A solo rendezvous with my Big God, and I mean in those private, hush-hush moments just like Matthew 6:6 advises. That's the foundation, sis. From there, the love and blessings flow to my church fam, my circle of Christian friends, and then out into the world. So, if you're down to align your life with what God truly values, Scripture's got a blueprint for us. It's a flow, starting with God and rippling out to everyone else. And when we get that order right, that's when our soul finds its peace, and our life starts to sing a big ol' hallelujah that the outside world simply can't ignore!

THE FAITH RIPPLE EFFECT: FROM INNER CIRCLE TO OUTER WORLD

Girl, have you ever tossed a stone into a pond and watched the ripples spread? I love doing that because it reminds me of how our faith should work. Stick with me; I've put together a visual that I hope

a gospel-centered approach to the

MINISTRY
Ripple-effect

STEP 1:
PERSONAL JESUS
ENCOUNTER

STEP 2:
FAMILY FIRST
MINISTRY

STEP 3:
INTIMATE GATHERINGS
*THIS INCLUDES OUTREACH TO THOSE JESUS
CALLS US TO REACH: THE LOW AND FORGOTTEN

STEP 4:
CHURCH IN THE MASSES + CROWDS

you'll vibe with as much I me. The idea is super simple but profound. Picture a circle with increasingly larger circles around it, kind of like ripples in the water. In the innermost circle is your private time with Jesus. That's where everything starts, right? This circle is non-negotiable; without it, the other circles don't even stand a chance. Jesus talks about this right?! He says something like this:

"Go into your room, shut the door and pray to your father who is in secret." Matthew 6:6-7 NIV

The second layer is your family. That's your first 'congregation,' so to speak. The health and happiness of your home life is the litmus test of how well your spiritual life is flourishing. We've got to be beacons of God's love right there at our own kitchen tables before we can shine that light anywhere else.

Then comes your spiritual squad. I'm talking about your close-knit Christian friends, your small interpersonal Bible study groups, and basically your ride-or-die kinda Jesus gals. This is where you get to apply all that you've learned in your inner circles, where you get to "walk your talk" in a broader but still personal setting. But guess what? This circle also is a means to commune with the "low and the forgotten" that Jesus was more often than not befriending. Here you get to really love on others in a more personal way that Jesus modeled.

The outermost circle? That's your public ministry. By the time you reach this circle, your actions will echo the love, grace, and wisdom you've nurtured in the inner circles.

So, that's the ripple effect of ministry. Each circle feeds into the next, making each subsequent circle stronger and more impactful. Trust me; it's the most practical way to ensure that your ministry is rooted in authentic faith and capable of far-reaching influence. Remember this: Jesus tells us explicitly that we are called to be faithful with the little before we can be faithful with much. So let's stay faithful to our smaller circles before we expand to the larger ones, y'all! It's as if Jesus knew we'd make a bigger impact—and see real change in ourselves and our community—by starting small. So don't go big right off the bat. Start with your inner circle, and let those love ripples grow from a solid core!

STARTING WITH YOU: YOUR ONE-ON-ONE WITH JESUS

Okay, ladies, let's talk. You know how self-care is all the rage these days? Well, your spiritual self-care starts with some one-on-one time with Jesus. Imagine it as a spa day for your soul, without the fancy robes and cucumber water. Jesus Himself made time to be alone and pray. So, if He needed it, you better believe we do too.

Now, flashback to my babysitting days—yes, even before Netflix made it cool. I've seen families that looked perfect on Instagram but were hot messes in real life. I'm talking about the ones who have Bible verses in their bio but chaos in their living rooms. It was like watching a real-life episode of a drama series, only without the popcorn. I once knew a woman, let's call her "Karen," who was all about that 'Bible study influencer' life. But behind those filtered selfies, girl, it was a different story. It was like she was living two lives—one for the 'Gram and one for, well, I don't know who. This taught me something big: we need to check ourselves before we start giving out spiritual advice like we're some life coaches. Now, I'm not throwing shade. We all have our moments. But this experience taught me something crucial: before you can be an inspiration to others, you have to get real with yourself and with God. A chaotic home often signals a chaotic spiritual life, and that's your cue to huddle up with God and get things right. I'm not here to judge; life is messy. But here's the tea: before we can give our best to our families, our friends, or anyone else, we've got to make sure we're spiritually grounded. So, if your home feels more like a battlefield than a sanctuary, maybe it's time for some divine intervention, you know? Grab that Bible, find a quiet spot, and let God do His thing. That sparkle ain't gonna come from ourselves but from the Holy Spirit within, girl (Matthew 6:6-8; Luke 5:16; Matthew 14:1-13; Luke 4:1-2, 14-15; Mark 6:30-32). So, after we've got our 'Jesus thang' back, it's time to sprinkle that love a little closer to home. So grab another cup of coffee—or wine, no judgment here.

STEP TWO IN OUR MINISTRY MODEL—PUTTING FAMILY FIRST

Y'all, Scripture isn't vague about this. Before we start leading Bible studies or taking on ministry roles, we need to make sure things are good at home. We're talking about soul-deep goodness—living truthfully, forgiving easily, and loving fiercely. Our homes, our families—they have to come first. Now, I'm not saying you need to have a Pinterest-perfect life, but there's got to be real, heartfelt connection at home. Why not make mealtime an "unplugged" holy moment? Share a verse, and while you're at it, ask the fam what they're praying for this week. Your living room can be a sanctuary for kindness, love, and good old-fashioned respect, all away from the spotlight. Trust me, there's no "Mom of the Year" award, but who cares? The real reward is a home full of love. The point is, our homes should be ground zero for showing love, respect, and gentleness. Most of this happens away from Instagram-worthy moments, just within the four walls of our home. No one's handing out trophies for being an amazing wife or mom, but let's be real: home is where the heart is. Our homes mirror our true selves. They show us who we really are and who we're becoming.

And honestly, it's the best place for God to work on making us into the loving, Christ-like people we want to be. This mutual ministry in the home isn't something we can opt out of if we want to grow in Christ. I've been rethinking what "church" means to me. It's less about big congregations and more about those precious moments at home. Our families are our first ministry, the folks God entrusted to us, y'all. And I believe my role as a wife, a mom, and a daughter of God starts right there, within my own four walls. Before we take our message of love and redemption out into the bigger world, we need to make sure our most intimate world—the home—is flourishing. Your home isn't just where you live; it's your first mission field. So, instead of running off to far-flung missions, what if we started with the mission field we wake up to every day? Why would we leave to do ministry elsewhere when our own little legacies could crumble because our kids aren't seeing a faith connection where it matters most—at home? (1 Timothy 5:8; 1 Timothy 3:5; Proverbs 17:17).

A QUICK NOTE FOR ALL THE SINGLE LADIES, COLLEGE GALS, AND WIFEYS WITHOUT KIDS

You might be thinking, "Well, I'm not a mom or a wife yet, so how does this apply to me?" Trust me, your home—whether it's a dorm room, a shared apartment, or just your personal space—is just as crucial. Your "family" could be your roommates, your sorority sisters, or even your close circle of friends. You have a sphere of influence right where you are. What about starting a weekly "Soulful Sunday" chat with your roomies where you all share a verse or spiritual insight? Or maybe you can be the one to break the ice on deep meaningful conversations when hanging out with your girlfriends. You don't have to be a mom to minister. Your current season of life provides unique opportunities to share God's love in a way that's just as impactful to the people you see and engage with intimately every single day. As a former socially anxious gal and social introvert, I understand that showing up in social settings can be challenging. However, experts suggest that stepping out of your comfort zone can have profound benefits. Studies have shown that pushing yourself to connect with others, even when it feels uncomfortable, can lead to improved health, increased lifespan and quality of life, reduced depression and anxiety in the long run, and boosted confidence. So, while it may take initiative and courage to show up, the connections you'll build will have lasting impacts, and your confidence will grow as you take steps and put yourself out there. I've noticed a significant transformation in my personality as I've embraced better connections with others. It's as if that old, socially anxious and shy girl wasn't my true personality but a result of sticking to my comfort zone for too long.

STEP THREE IN OUR MINISTRY MODEL—CHURCH AROUND THE TABLE

Ready for the next ripple in this ministry wave? Let's talk about the role of the table in Jesus' ministry, which is so overlooked yet so powerful. We see in the Bible that some of Jesus' most touching moments happened around a table. It was around tables that His friends truly got to know Him. He didn't just use the table for a meal; He used it as a teaching moment, a place for vulnerability, celebration, and meeting needs—physical, emotional, and spiritual. Now, you might say, "Okay, so Jesus loved a good meal with friends. What's the big deal?" But think about it. The table was more than just a place for food; it was a symbol for intimacy and deep connection. So, if we're aiming to lead lives filled with purpose, we can't skip out on deep, real relationships with those who share our faith and values. We were created for this kind of relational depth—we're meant to truly connect, to "go there" with each other. So, maybe the next step for you is inviting some friends over for a casual dinner, breaking bread, and diving into deep conversations about life and faith. It's about making church less about a building and more about a living, breathing community that you foster right in your home. [Mark 2:15; Luke 7:36; Matthew 26:26; Luke 7:34; Matthew 11:19; Matthew 9:10; John 21:12; John 12:2; Luke 24:29-31; Luke 24:43].

Speaking of living, breathing communities and being faithful in small acts, let me share something personal with you. You know how they say, "Be faithful in the little things"? It's actually straight from the Bible: "Whoever can be trusted with very little can also be trusted with much" (Luke 16:10, NIV). I had this nudge from the Lord to start a widows ministry. All jazzed up and ready to roll, I shared my grand plan with my husband. And you know what he said? "Why not start with the widow right here?" Talk about a gospel mic drop.

Sometimes, we get so fired up to do grand things for the Lord—often up on a big platform with lots of production and attention—that we forget what Mother Teresa so beautifully said:

❝

"There are no great things, only small things with great love."

Isn't that just echoing what the Bible tells us? "If I have a faith that can move mountains, but do not have love, I am nothing" (1 Corinthians 13:2 NIV).

So, here's my heart-to-heart for you, just as my husband had for me: Start small. Look for the 'one,' not the 'many.' Pour your heart and soul into that 'one' place where it's unseen, just like how Jesus left the ninety-nine to find that one lost sheep (Luke 15:4 NIV). It's like playing a heavenly game of hide-and-seek—hide from your right hand what your left hand is doing. Then, your Father, "who sees what is done in secret, will reward you" (Matthew 6:4 NIV). That's the kind of faithfulness that pleases the Lord, and trust me, it creates ripple effects much more significant than spreading yourself thin trying to love the masses.

So, in the name of not forsaking the 'one' for the 'many,' let's remember to keep our love genuine and our efforts laser-focused. Because in the grand scheme of God's plan, it's the small acts of great love that truly move mountains.

STEP FOUR IN OUR MINISTRY MODEL- CHURCH IN MASSES

Eager to set off the next ripple in our ministry pond? Let's get at it, ladies! You know how we cherish those big Sunday services, right? The music, the community, and that collective 'Amen!' It's all good, but let's dive into what Christianity Today noted about how Jesus himself dealt with crowds. They put it like this: "Jesus didn't value crowds. He didn't even trust them (John 2:23-24). But he valued the people in them…Even though they chased Him everywhere He went, Jesus and crowds had, at best, a strained relationship. Jesus didn't turn the crowds away when they found Him. But He sometimes made Himself hard to find."[10]

There is a place to gather together in large groups, to outreach, serve, or to worship collectively and to pray. This can be a great encouragement to our faith. But as Jesus modeled during nearly every encounter we see in Scripture between Jesus and a crowd, Jesus always retreated to go off alone by Himself. The crowds wore Jesus out. But I believe that the crowds were also not His primary mission field. The takeaway? The gathering of the masses is not a replacement to our personal relationship with Jesus, family-first ministry, and church done intimately one-on-one, and in small groups—authentically and vulnerably.

What's the takeaway here? Big Sunday services are uplifting, but they don't replace the personal, everyday walks with Jesus. These services should not be the only way we engage with our faith from week to week. Just like Jesus, who often retreated to recharge, we need to find our quiet corners too.

So, two big things: First, take your big group vibes and sprinkle them into smaller, more intimate settings throughout your week. Maybe it's a deep dive into scripture with your BFFs over coffee, or a laid-back prayer sesh at home. Secondly, let's own our faith. Listen to that inner guide—the Holy Spirit—and use it to navigate your own spiritual journey.

Ladies, being a woman of God means being proactive about your spiritual health. It's about having the discernment to be your own moral compass, so you can navigate life's challenges without losing your way. So if you're going to be around people, be all there; but remember, being with God is where you recharge. Keep that balance, and you won't just be riding the wave—you'll be making your own ripples.

A HEARTFELT NOTE ON FINDING THE RIGHT CHURCH FAMILY

Okay, my beautiful souls, can I just say how much I'm loving our heart-to-heart? Let's keep this soulful convo going, shall we? If you're like me, you know how invigorating a soul-stirring Sunday service can be. But let's have some real talk—there's no such thing as a picture-perfect church. Why? Because we, the beautifully flawed humans who make up the congregation, are far from perfect. Right? Now, this is crucial: knowing this simple truth can arm us against the not-so-holy forces that roam both inside and outside of church sanctuaries. Yep, the spiritual warfare doesn't stop at the church door! In fact, it's just getting started!

So, how do we find 'The One'? No, not your soulmate—your soul sanctuary! Well, here are the game-changers: the teachings, the vibe of the pastor, and oh yes—the internal church politics. These elements can either make your faith flourish like a blooming flower or wilt it away. The goal isn't to find a church that's perfect (because none is); instead, we're looking for two key things:

◊ A church where you can feel God's presence in every nook and cranny

◊ A pastoral team that's humble and actually invites God to take the reins.

Decision time shouldn't be a spur-of-the-moment thing, lovelies. Dive deep into prayer, and let God's voice be louder than your own thoughts. Research the church's beliefs and check if they align with the Bible. A quick visit to the church's website usually spills the tea!

What about scheduling a coffee catch-up with the pastor? Ask about his faith journey, his current walk with God, and just get a vibe check on his spiritual level. And here's a pro tip: attend one of those "New Member Meetings" to get the lowdown from other church leaders. Remember, we're biblically advised to be picky about our spiritual leaders.

Last but never least, tune into your spirit. If you're not feeling peace or joy, God might be gently nudging you away. On the flip side, when you sense peace flooding over you like a wave, you're probably onto something good.

With that said, lovelies, let's protect our peace, our faith, and especially our little ones. Not every church leader is ordained by our Good God. Let's be smart about where we plant ourselves to grow. And as a side note: even if he is ordained by God, remember this: not everything he says and in fact some of what he says is GUARANTEED to not be in tune with the Spirit- cuz sis, he ain't perfect! So check your spirit before and after service and ask the Lord to give you discernment, girl. This is like SO important. Sending you all love and prayers on your church-hunting and church-planting journey!

A SOULFUL CONVERSATION ABOUT THE SABBATH: A DAY TO BREATHE, NOT HUSTLE

Can we switch gears and have a conversation about something that's been on my heart—the idea of rest? I want us to take a step back and evaluate things, really. Our modern-day church life, especially in those colossal mega-churches, often feels like a relentless rat race. But pause and ask yourself: Is that what Jesus had in mind for us?

Spoiler alert: It's a big, fat "No!"

We're often caught up doing church in a way that exhausts us and ignores what Jesus truly cherishes. He values precious time with the Lord, intimate moments with family, genuine friendships, and—we can't forget—rest and peace. Get this, darlings: the Sabbath was God's gift to us, not to Himself. He designed it to rejuvenate us; think of it as our 'Shabbat Shalom,' our peace day! Worship and community on this holy day should recharge us, not deplete us. You know how Jesus pulled away from the crowds to rest? Well, I've been following His lead by leaning into smaller, more intimate circles, and let me tell you—it's a game-changer. Maybe you could try it too?

IN A WORLD FULL OF MARTHAS, IT'S OKAY TO BE A MARY!

Do you remember the story of Mary and Martha? Martha was bustling around, stressed to the max, while Mary simply sat at Jesus' feet. When Martha complained, Jesus gently told her, "Mary has chosen what is better, and it will not be taken away from her" (Luke 10:40 NIV).

Ever felt like you were on a spiritual treadmill, hustling for God's favor? I've been there. My Martha tendencies made me wonder why all my frantic doing wasn't making me feel closer to God. Then it clicked. God was saying, "You're so busy for me, but you don't actually know me." This wake-up call shifted something in me. Instead of staying perpetually busy, I've been letting God whisper to my soul in the still, quiet mornings. Like Mary, I've realized this might raise some eyebrows in our Martha-dominated church culture. And you know what? That's A-OK. As I've meditated with the Lord in the mornings, He's been gently whispering to my soul that I need rest. Like Mary, I've come to understand that finding rest in the Lord will inevitably ruffle some feathers, especially among the Marthas of the religious world. And that's okay. You see, I used to be a Martha too. Even now, I often feel that Martha-like urge to take control creeping back in.

However, I constantly remind myself that the truly important things in life can't be hurried or perfected; they must be fully enjoyed with my undivided attention. Whether it's quality time with Jesus, cherishing moments with my 4-year-old, rare yet intentional moments alone with my husband, or the close-knit fellowship within my church community, these are the aspects of life that deserve my full presence. I aspire to be a good Christian and to be effective in spreading the Gospel. Despite my best efforts, Jesus has been showing me that I can achieve these goals without the constant hustle. That I can maintain my sanity, find peace, and create room for my soul to breathe. Admittedly, I've fallen short of experiencing the Gospel's fullness, both in what I give and what I receive. I'm now course-correcting this by stepping back from the church building to nurture my own individual faith first, then extending that faith into my home, and beyond. The more I follow this path, the clearer it becomes that I answer only to Christ. When my earthly journey ends, and I stand before Jesus, it will be Him alone to whom I must answer. He will measure how well I've stewarded my faith, cared for my loved ones, and ministered to my community.

What's become increasingly apparent is that God doesn't tally my worth by numbers or by how many souls I've "saved." The Kingdom of God is measured by love. On the day I stand before God, He will assess how loving and intentional I've been (1 Corinthians 13:2). Hence, I am striving for quality in my faith journey, not quantity.

So, let's not forget that God measures our faith by the love we give, not the numbers we reach. The Apostle Paul puts it perfectly, "If I speak with human eloquence and angelic ecstasy but don't love, I'm nothing but the creaking of a rusty gate. If I speak God's Word with power, revealing all his mysteries and making everything plain as day, and if I have faith that says to a mountain, "Jump," and it jumps, but I don't love, I'm nothing. If I give everything I own to the poor and even go to the stake to be burned as a martyr, but I don't love, I've gotten nowhere. So, no matter what I say, what I believe, and what I do, I'm bankrupt without love." (1 Corinthians 13:1-7 MSG). That's the ultimate mic drop, isn't it? So, loves, let's make space for God, cherish those close to us, and embrace the beauty of rest. I promise, when you focus on the quality of your faith instead of just the numbers, your soul will be singing thank you notes. The ripple effects of your glowing ministry will be so crystal clear, the world will take notice and crave what you've got. It's like a refreshing breeze in a world obsessed with the hustle, but coming up empty and short. Everyone will want what you've got!

A FULL CUP: MY JOURNEY FROM SPIRITUAL EXHAUSTION TO OVERFLOWING GRACE

Sis, if I can be real with you, there was a time when I felt like I was always playing catch-up in my spiritual life. I found myself consumed by the church building—the activities, the people, the sermons, and everything in between. But a profound realization struck me: I needed to recalibrate my priorities. God had to come first. To make room for Him, I intentionally cut out distractions that took me away from what truly mattered. Let me tell you, the dividends this has paid in my spiritual life, as well as my overall well-being, have been beyond amazing. Don't get me wrong; the church building is more than bricks and mortar. It's a meeting ground, a hub of worship, a space to engage with the Word. But you know what? It's not where your spiritual journey begins and ends. When you are committed to daily nourishment—feasting on the Bread of Life and spending quality time with God—you come to Sunday service with a full cup. You're not there to fill up; you're there to pour out love and service from an already brimming reservoir of grace. This shift in perspective does wonders. It puts the Great Commission into context. We can better manage God's blessings in our lives and teach our children to do the same. Our tight-knit community keeps us anchored and accountable, transforming church into a sanctuary where true worship in Spirit and truth is a collective experience.

Look, the church has been a cornerstone for me. I met my husband there; I forged deep friendships there. It's been the backdrop for many of God's miracles in my life. Yet, it's also where I've battled spiritual confusion, encountered fear-mongering from the pulpit, been abused, and wrestled with teachings that disconnected rather than connected me with Christ.

We often think that it's among the broken congregation that we find Jesus. While there's some truth to that, let's not forget that Jesus Himself pulled away from the crowds for intimate communion with the Father. It's in these quiet moments away from the clamor that we can be most effectively filled by God, preparing us to serve and be served in the wider community. So, in closing, church is beautiful, but God calls us into a deeper relationship with Him— one that transcends the pews and alters. A full cup doesn't just happen; it's the product of a life lived in deliberate communion with God. Trust me, when your cup is full, not only will your soul thank you, but you'll also find a greater purpose and joy in the community of believers around you.

LET'S SPILL THE TEA:

We're doing a Deep Dive into the Gospel Ripple Effect. Let's have a heart to heart, sis.

INNERMOST CIRCLE: YOUR ONE-ON-ONE TIME WITH JESUS

> **Heart Space:** How are you carving out sacred moments to sit, undisturbed, with Jesus? Is there anything that keeps these moments rare rather than routine?

> **Soulful Echo:** After you've had that treasured time with Jesus, how does it ripple through your emotions, decisions, and conversations for the day?

> **Core Connection:** Does the ripple effect resonate with you at a heart level? Do you feel a deep link between the quality of your time with Jesus and the ripple impact it has on other layers of your life?

SECOND LAYER: YOUR FAMILY

> **Sanctuary at Home:** Have you ever looked around your dinner table and realized that these faces are your first ministry? How does that revelation sit in your heart?

> **Daily Grace:** Can you think of tender ways to weave spiritual conversations into the simple daily rituals at home? Over breakfast smoothies or bedtime stories perhaps?

> **Walking the Talk:** Do you know someone who is the epitome of grace in public but a storm cloud at home? How does that disconnect touch your heart? How do you think it touches Jesus'?

THIRD LAYER: YOUR SPIRITUAL TRIBE

> **Kindred Spirits:** Who fills your spiritual circle with love, faith, and wisdom? How do you mutually enrich each other's soul journey?

> **Ah-Ha Moments:** Share a heartwarming memory when your spiritual tribe was the balm to your soul.

FOURTH LAYER: PUBLIC MINISTRY

> **Radical Love:** Jesus was explicit in modeling a ministry that focuses on the poor, the orphans, and the widows. After all, "It is not the healthy who need a doctor, but the sick" (Matthew 9:12-13). How is your heart being nudged to step outside the church 'building' and channel your love and service toward those Jesus deeply cared for?

> **World Stage:** How are you taking your faith and love to the broader world? Does it bring your heart joy?

> **Community vs. Checklist:** Have you ever felt that church involvement seemed more like a to-do list than a community of love?

> **Inner vs. Outer:** Do you ever find yourself giving so much

to the outer layers that your inner sanctuary feels neglected? How does that weigh on your soul?

GENERAL SOUL-SEARCHING QUESTIONS ON THE GOSPEL RIPPLE EFFECT

> **Safe Haven:** Which circle feels like a warm hug to your spirit, and why?

> **Harmony or Dissonance:** Ever feel like one circle is in a sweet harmony while another is a little off-key? How are you thinking of tuning that?

FOR SINGLE LADIES, COLLEGE GALS, AND WIFEYS WITHOUT KIDS

> **Your Unique Melody:** How are you customizing this model to dance to the beat of your own life stage?

> **The Heart of Influence:** Where do you see room for more love, more grace, and more Gospel in your current life?

IF YOU WANT TO CHANGE THE WORLD GO HOME AND LOVE YOUR FAMILY

MOTHER THERESA

19

THE WILDERNESS EXPERIENCE:

A Sisterly Chat for Women on a Soulful Journey

"

Don't dig up in doubt what you planted in faith. – Elisabeth Elliot

O h, my lovelies, have you ever found yourself clinging to your Bible, maybe even peeling at its worn edges when you're deep in thought? My own Bible is a treasured mess— its faux leather is chipping away, and the purple pen marks have matured into a soft bubblegum pink over time. I've read the Gospels a gazillion times back and forth. But, just like a comforting chat over tea with your go-to girlfriend, it never fails to reveal something new that reaches the untouched corners of my heart. I never cease to be amazed at how new meanings can jump out at me, cutting straight to my heart. I love that. I love that we can read the same verse repeatedly, yet God can still scrape at untouched depths. This is what happens when we read through Scripture with the Spirit. It comes alive, acting as medicine to our bones and counseling for our souls. It's comforting in all the ways a best friend can be when you need her most.

Speaking of friends, a friend and I recently committed to reading and studying the entire Bible together. So here I am, reading through the book of Mark for the thousandth time. I began with Mark 1 last week, almost taking it for granted because I knew exactly where the Apostle Mark was headed; I had it memorized. But I felt as if I had some sort of spiritual lens on, because what used to just be a recounting of Jesus' baptism became rich in meaning for me. Let's read the first part of Mark together:

The Baptism of Jesus

In those days, Jesus came from Nazareth of Galilee and was baptized by John in the Jordan. And when He came up out of the water, immediately He saw the heavens being torn open and the Spirit descending on Him like a dove. A voice came from heaven, "You are my beloved Son; with you, I am well pleased."

The Spirit immediately drove Him out into the wilderness.

He was in the wilderness for forty days, being tempted by Satan. He was with the wild animals, and the angels were ministering to Him.

Jesus Begins His Ministry. Mark 1:9-13 ESV (Italics mine.)

Did you catch that? Jesus was baptized in the Holy Spirit and immediately went into the wilderness to fast and pray. He was being led into the wilderness to connect with His Father in spirit and truth. He didn't go to the synagogue or the temple, and He didn't start His ministry until after He spent forty days and nights alone with His Father-God! There were essential things to be done among the crowds and those who believed, and Jesus knew that. However, He also knew that His true power rested in the Father and that He could accomplish nothing without Him. So His first priority was to get in tune with the Father's heart. And then what did He do? He went and found His people, His ride-or-die buddies, His twelve!

Sweet souls, I believe we all similarly go through a wilderness experience after receiving the Spirit of God upon salvation—if we truly lean in with a desire to know and be known by the Father, like Jesus did. It might come years later, after we've strayed only to return to God like the prodigal daughter, desperate for comfort, food, and a welcoming hug. This was my experience.

I was saved at the age of seven. I attended church, prayed, and tried to live righteously before the God who had so graciously saved me. But seven is a young age to fully grasp the realities of His kingdom, here on Earth as it is in Heaven. I did my best, Lord knows I did, ya'll. Yet my faith never truly integrated into the fabric of my life until, like the prodigal son, I decided to come home. I turned thirteen and was desperate for an anchor in my life. I recommitted to Christ, was baptized (three times, just for good measure), and entered my own wilderness experience with God. However, mine didn't last 40 days like our perfect Messiah. My wilderness period lasted 10 years. Like the Israelites leaving Egypt for the Promised Land, I had a lot of healing to do, sins to overcome, and a faith that needed to become my own. During those ten years in the wilderness, God was sanctifying me and drawing my heart toward Him in spirit and truth. It was—and still is—necessary for me to spend time alone with the Father when I want to lean into His Spirit. While the church community is important, the religion I've often encountered within the structure and tradition of the church building has sometimes hindered my wilderness experience. The soul work that God needs to do in us can only happen when we get alone with Him in the wilderness and lean in. I believe we all need to embrace this wilderness experience alone with God to gain a proper spiritual foundation. Now, I'm not saying that I never set foot in a church or sought the wisdom of pastors or those mature in their faith. But during this wilderness period, I spent hours each day with the Lord. I fasted, prayed, studied Scripture, journaled, and got alone with God every single day for ten years. I was desperate to know God and be known by Him.

What I'm saying, sis, is that there is an order to things when we come to know Jesus, and it starts with Jesus himself. This happens alone and in quiet places. Without this foundation in the wilderness, alone with Jesus, we cannot develop the discernment that comes from a close, everyday walk with the Lord.

THE 11-DAY JOURNEY THAT LASTED 40 YEARS: LESSONS FROM THE ISRAELITES' WILDERNESS EXPERIENCE

Okay sis, let's talk about a pretty crazy wilderness experience that we can often gloss over in Sunday school. Can we just talk about the Israelites, ya'll? Can you believe the Israelites spent 40 years in the wilderness when it was only an eleven-day journey from Mount

Sinai to Kadesh-barnea, AKA the Promised Land? Yep, you heard that right, sis—eleven days! Deuteronomy 1:2-3 lays it out: what should've been a less than two-week trip turned into a lifetime for a whole generation. They spent 40 years going in circles because they couldn't trust and obey a loving God. So tragic, right? Because of their lack of trust and, therefore, obedience in a good God, the entire original generation that left Egypt never even got to set foot in the Promised Land. They died off, wandering aimlessly, never reaching that place of promise. Heart-wrenching, huh, sis?

Now, let's keep it real. We can be like those wandering Israelites, too. We get stuck in cycles of mistrust and fear, because of past hurts or mistakes. Our hearts harden, and before we know it, we're in a never-ending loop of what-ifs and if-onlys.

But listen, beautiful, here's the game-changer: You've got a heavenly Father who wants nothing but the best for you. He's ready to lead you out of your personal wilderness and into a life of promise. A life where your ashes turn into beauty, where wounds find healing, and where what's broken gets restored. But it's going to take trust and obedience in our good God to finally arrive.

So let's do this, okay? Lean into God, trust His heart for you, and take that step into your Promised Land. Your future self will thank you for it!

FROM SHAKY GROUND TO SOLID ROCK: CULTIVATING YOUR PERSONAL FAITH IN AN IMPERFECT WORLD

What's that look like? Oh, I'm so glad you asked. We must discipline ourselves to spend time alone with God in the quiet places where He ministers to our hearts. A strong faith in God is highly individual before it becomes communal. We need to develop our own convictions. We must learn to discern truth for ourselves. We need deliverance from sin, which is genuinely self-harm. We need healing from generational strongholds, childhood wounds, and traumas. We need to become whole in Christ and invite Him into every area of our lives. God even invites us to bring our dreams and desires before Him repeatedly. But regardless, we need to be grounded in who Christ is to us personally so that even when the church fails, and when flawed truths are shared, and people fail to meet our expectations, our faith remains strong because it's founded on the unshakeable Christ. Any other foundation is sinking sand.

We can't give the keys or even the authority over our faith to any church, pastor, life group leader, or mentor. Our faith, beliefs, and convictions must be our own. They must be developed in the secret places where we pray, read the Scriptures with the Spirit, fast, and grow closer to the Spirit of God within us. Any other authority given over is a recipe for spiritual chaos and disorder that can affect all other aspects of our wholeness and health. Of course, a community of carefully-vetted believers can and should speak into our lives. We should be surrounded by strong Christians who hold us accountable, and we should do the same for them. But this must be done carefully, through prayer and discernment. There is no room for laziness if we are to build a strong spiritual foundation for our figurative chairs that stand firm in the day of trouble.

I want to leave you with this: When Jesus was asked which of the commandments was the greatest, He didn't hesitate to reply: "Love the Lord your God with all your heart and with all your soul and with all your mind and with all your strength.' The second is this: 'Love your neighbor as yourself.' There is no commandment greater than these." (Mark 12:30-31). If we don't first learn to love God in spirit and in truth, we can't fully love ourselves or anyone else. And in that moment, when asked about the greatest commandment, Jesus is teaching us what we need to know to prepare our hearts to serve Him and others effectively. So, dear sister, hear me out. To truly experience the full spectrum of God's shalom—in our minds, bodies, spirits, and deep in our soul—we must prioritize our wilderness experience. Before our faith life can be a shared journey, it must first be a personal and authentic pilgrimage. Seize your wilderness, and there find the rest that your soul so earnestly seeks.

LET'S SPILL THE TEA, SIS!

> **Well-Worn Bible:** Okay, spill the tea, sis! Is your Bible a "treasured mess" too? How has your love for Scripture matured over time?

> **Spiritual Lens:** Ever stumble upon a sparkling new gem in a Bible passage you thought you knew like the back of your hand? What flicked the spiritual light switch for you?

> **The Jesus Route:** Have you ever found yourself led by the Spirit into a wilderness experience like Jesus? What did you learn during that time?

> **The Prodigal Daughter:** Have you had your prodigal daughter moment, where you had no choice but to run back into God's loving arms? How did your understanding of God's grace change during that season?

> **40 Days vs. 10 Years:** Have you experienced a prolonged wilderness season that seemed never to end? What kept you going?

> **Trust Issues:** The Israelites took 40 years for what could have been an eleven-day journey. Are there areas in your life where lack of trust is delaying your arrival at your "Promised Land"?

> **The Obedience Factor:** Can you identify a moment where your obedience to God accelerated your journey out of the wilderness?

> **The Game-Changer:** Come on, beautiful soul. What could change if you fully leaned into trusting God's heart for you?

> **Authentic Pilgrimage:** How can you ensure that your faith remains your own, unaffected by others' opinions or interpretations?

> **The Greatest Commandment:** How are you currently loving God with all your heart, soul, mind, and strength? What steps can you take to align more closely with this commandment?

20

WHY FOLLOW THE CROWD

When You Can Follow The Creator?

"

Once upon a time, I thought that my faith and my happy place were two worlds apart. But as it turns out, they were soul-sisters all along.

You've heard the saying, 'out with the old, in with the new,' right? But how often do we hesitate to push that reset button in our lives? We clutch our old beliefs, habits, and attitudes, fearing what might happen if we let go—even when they're dragging us down. Sound familiar?

I was one of those people, trapped by teachings from my church that placed happiness and faith in opposing corners. They had me convinced that a deep, emotional connection with God was off-limits. And let me tell you, they couldn't have been more wrong.

Today, my faith isn't just a part of me—it fills me with so much love and joy that I can't help but share it. My happiness isn't something I've found in people-pleasing or relentless striving. Instead, it's rooted in a divine love that has transformed my life in ways I never thought possible. And guess what? It's a love that's emotional, vibrant, and overflowing.

WELCOME TO THE WORLD OF GOSPEL BEAUTIFULL

I used to pride myself on being a self-made woman, overcoming life's obstacles through sheer grit and determination. But here's the kicker: this place of abundance that I am at today isn't the result of me pulling myself up by the ol' bootstraps. It's the result of God's transformative love, guidance, and the grace that rained down when I needed it most. And yes, it was me leaning in and submitting to His good ways. I can say this, sis, what was once a life struggling in the wilderness has blossomed into my very own Promised Land. I've come home to a faith that's emotional, deep, and, dare I say, beautiful. So, to anyone who feels stuck, who thinks their current reality is all there is, let me offer you this: hit that reset button. Clear the clutter and make room for a faith that doesn't just exist—it thrives. Welcome to the world of Gospel Beautifull.

BLINDSIDED BY BLIND SPOTS: MY REAL TALK TESTIMONY

So, listen, let's chat a little bit more before we wrap up this soul-to-soul convo that I've been enjoying so much. Ever feel like you're playing the never-ending game of needing everyone's approval? Trust me, like I've said, I've been there. For the longest time, I was caught up in this religious loop of approval, transactional love, and the quest for perfection. You wanna know why? These weren't new habits; they were old wounds, scars from my past that never healed. Yep, they were my blind spots, lessons from life that I hadn't fully understood yet. I carried these insecurities from my childhood right into adulthood, wrapping them in a veneer of faith. I'd lived in that mindset my whole life, seeking validation from any corner I could find it—not just in church but everywhere. It's like we're conditioned this way, not just by faith but by the world around us too. Our human nature resists the idea of self-correction, so instead, we reshape God to fit into our own little boxes, marked by our flawed ideologies and experiences.

Did you even know there are over 200 types of Christianity in the U.S. and over 45,000 worldwide? Insane, right? We make God's simple, graceful love so complicated that we create whole denominations just to make sense of it all. **But here's what I've come to realize: Why follow the crowd when you can follow the Creator?**

Now, the honest truth: Nobody, and I mean nobody, has it all figured out (1 Corinthians 13:9-12 NIV). Whether you're a fashionista or a plain Jane, we're all fumbling through life. The imposter syndrome is universal, girl. Let's cut ourselves and each other some slack, okay? Here's the real tea: the only approval that matters is God's. It took me a long time to grasp that, but now my daily connection with God is as routine as my morning coffee. What we really need is a sprinkle of Jesus in our lives (and a cup of coffee doesn't hurt either, let's be real). So that's it, sis. My journey has taught me to keep it simple, to keep it real, and just to be me—with God by my side. And trust me, if I can do it, you can too.

THE WAY TO TRUE LIFE

I am saying that in order to be whole and find life, beautiful and felt, we've got to throw off the more and get to the uncluttered, unburied, bare heart of where that life is really to be found. And Jesus says this: "I am the way the truth and the life, no one comes to the father except through me" (John 14:6). I've come to find for myself that Jesus isn't found in the church noise, service at the coffee bars, or by volunteering in the nursery on Sundays. And He certainly isn't found by placing ourselves under the teaching of world renowned speakers, preachers, or those we think know so much more than us. If the church is the primary place we are going for our Jesus experience, we are not going to be whole or full in Christ. The Church as we do it on Sunday must be supplemental to our own intentional walk with the Lord, family-focused ministry, and small-knit group of believers that we authentically connect with on a regular basis.

What I've found through my lifetime spent in the religion of the evangelical church and what I want to share with you, dear sis, is this: I have been taught an incomplete gospel. The common day evangelical church is built upon half of the gospel where we get saved to go out and "do" but we miss the gospel that is for us and in us! The Holy Spirit came to save us, to come live in us, and change us. Not just for the sake of others, but for you and me, personally.

TRANSFORMED: FINDING PEACE AND WHOLENESS IN A WORLD OF CHAOS

The more I grow apart from religion and the world, and the more I grow in tune with God through prayer and divine encounters morning by morning, the more I feel I'm being thrust into all that God intended for me to be. I like who I am. I'm finding my wholeness and mental health. New and old passions alike are rising up within me. A quietness, too, is settling in my soul. There is a peace within me now that not only can I feel, but family members are asking me what I've done. "What have you changed? You seem like a new kind of person over the past year." What they mean is that my life-or-death battle with depression is gone. My anxious and bitter heart has grown three times its size. The strongholds that used to drown out the most precious parts of me are now healed, in Jesus' name.

I feel that I have been given a new life altogether—a redo without all the gunk in my soul that was keeping me from the inner peace that I've always been after. My father-in-law has noted the change in me. My sister has noticed it as well. My husband has cried and told me that for so long he has prayed for my healing and wholeness, specifically! He just sent me a text the other day that reads,

"I am so, so proud of you. I'm so proud that my eyes are tearing up as I write this. I'm so in love with you, Maddisen. You have changed so much in the past year, and it just amazes me what you've healed from! I feel like you are a different person, but I always knew who you were at the core when I married you. I could see beyond the trauma and the pain and the fear and the rough exterior into who you were beneath all that. You have fought like hell to get where you are today, and I'm so grateful that you've done the hard work that people rarely do in order to get free. My love for you is just growing and growing. You're so special, Maddisen; you have no idea."

I wanted to share that with you because I could sit here and write a whole book on how to live the Christian life. But at the end of the day, if it doesn't really change my own life, then it doesn't mean a thing. If my own family, first—my husband and son—are not blessed and positively affected by my supposed walk with the Lord, then what is the point? Really?!

FINDING BEAUTY IN LIFE'S IMPERFECTIONS

I want to emphasize that life's journey isn't a linear one. It's more like a graph, filled with its ups and downs. My husband, Vincent, often reminds me that there will be good days and challenging days, but as long as we lean on the Lord and seek His strength, we'll consistently trend upward.

The enemy, particularly during times of loss, hardship, or challenging days, loves to be an accuser, whispering that these struggles and even our past struggles define who we are. However, I know the truth. I am a beloved daughter of the King, and He has incredible plans for me. My identity is not tethered to my past battles with depression and anxiety or whatever I've gone through.

I also want to encourage you, dear reader. Even if you've conquered challenges or received deliverance from them, don't be disheartened if they reappear in your life during difficult times. Keep moving forward, speak truth over yourself, and remember that the Lord has redeemed you, and you're not regressing.

I often liken my past struggles to the story of Sodom and Gomorrah. It's tempting to look back, similar to Lot's wife, seeking comfort in what used to be, foolish as that may sound. But, like her, we always have a choice. Do we obey the Lord and continue moving toward His plans for us, or do we dwell on what's proven destructive in our lives, becoming frozen like a pillar of salt? My consistent choice is to look forward, toward the good plans the Lord has in store for me, and to lean into Him during moments of pain, relying on Him as my source of strength.

What I want you to know, beautiful reader, is that your own journey to wholeness and beauty in Christ isn't a flawless, straight path; we never fully arrive. You may reach a point one day, only for life to knock you down, reminding you of your unwavering foundation in Christ. Sometimes, life isn't so beautiful, right? But we can always find beauty in it when our foundation is in Christ.

Don't be discouraged if you overcome trials in life, only to feel like you've circled back to the starting line down the road. You haven't reached the destination yet, but you're making progress, and you're not the same person today as you were yesterday. Remember that, dear friend. All we can do is keep looking to Christ and trust that He is leading us forward, even when the path seems challenging.

FROM ASHES TO BEAUTY: A JOURNEY TO WHOLENESS THROUGH GOD'S GRACE

I want you to know that authentic wholeness and happiness in Christ are real, and they're available to you. And yes, it's going to take work and it's not going to be perfect. But it's worth it.

Seeing my life as it is now is surreal. I've been taking note of where I am versus where I used to be. I've been building somewhat of a memorial to the faithfulness of my God, just like Jacob did, so that I will never forget what my God has done for me. My life has gone from ashes to beauty. God has repaid me for the years the locusts have eaten. He has placed me, once so lonely, in a family. He has redeemed my life and given me a song to sing—a song of God's faithfulness and profound Abba-Father love for me.

My life isn't perfect, but it's a story with its own kind of beauty. And let me tell you, I would not be where I am today if I were still locked up in the legalism of religion, still trapped in the spaces of my church-going good-girl ways that didn't want to disappoint or disagree. If I had stayed too scared to go my own way and travel alone, I would still be bound and shackled. I would still be mired in my paralyzing depression and my panic attacks—my purposelessness and my fear. My locked-jaw control and my head-spinning busyness. Change was necessary. A little TLC was needed. Getting my priorities in check was freeing. Learning that I don't need to ask permission was incredibly empowering. And giving myself permission to stay in my lane was life-giving.

I'm learning to live a fuller life—a more present one. My faith no longer looks the same. My family looks different too. My calendar has changed. My abused and overactive conscience has been set free. I'm different. And everything is so much better for it. Going the way of the crowd, it turns out, was like being walked on a chain—collar fixed around my neck, spikes turning inward should I move out of the status quo or defy what is approved by the masses. It was torturing me. My soul couldn't take it anymore. I had to escape, no matter the cost. And it turns out, the cost wasn't much—other than leaving behind the religious world that I'm now so glad I left. I've lost a few fair-weather friends and received a few disapproving looks. But what I've gained is so much more! I've gained health and wellness in my spirit, mind, body, and soul. I am whole, for the first time in my life.

THE ROAD LESS TRAVELED: FINDING MY TRIBE AND MY TRUE NORTH IN GOD

Everything I initially came to the church to fix in myself as a child,

God has now done for me. I've regained a piece of my inner child, but I've also grown so much that I almost don't recognize the broken person I used to be. I'm closer to God, my husband, and my son, and I've made friends who are perfectly imperfect—people who enrich my life because they are genuine. I finally have the group of friends I've always wanted—the kind I can call up in the middle of the night crying, and it's not awkward. The deepest, most valuable aspects of my life are incredibly fulfilling. So, I'd say I'm heading in the right direction. I think I'll stay on this road less traveled; I like it too much to go back to following the crowd.

Sometimes my days are unproductive, and sometimes I disconnect from important tasks to connect personally with God. The laundry might go undone, and the house could be a mess. There are days when my four-year-old wanders around the house in just underwear—or sometimes we don't even make it to that. We don't attend church on Sundays anymore; instead, we are in a season where we're letting God guide us. Perhaps someday we'll find the right Christ-led church building to call home. But for now, I am home, right where God wants me to be. In obedience to our call to not neglect fellowship with other believers, we've traded the empty busyness of our local church for a small group of people with whom we study the Word together. I'm not saying this is how you should do it; it's just how we do it.

Our life group has been a lifeline to us in more ways than one, but that hasn't come without intentionality, authenticity, and consistency. We have a group chat where we stay connected throughout the week, discussing peculiar questions like, "Hey, should I tip a stylist who works from her home?" (By the way, I still don't know the answer to that question, but I do anyways.) We share prayer requests for sick children or family members facing life-threatening diseases. We exchange used baby clothes and offer babysitting. We engage in Bible studies and game nights, celebrate Friendsgiving and Christmas potlucks, we host Galentines brunches, and otherwise dine together at the gospel table. We strive to stay as connected as possible in a busy world where both our families and personal faith are priorities—until the next girls' game night, playdate, co-joined family vacation, or dinner around the table, where we can connect authentically.

IN HINDSIGHT

If I could time-travel, I would go back to my seven-year-old self and invite her to dine with me at my table. I'd prepare my favorite meal: pumpkin cream gnocchi. This dish has become my go-to when I'm hosting church around my table. It's a simple but delightful blend of gnocchi, heavy cream, caramelized onions, thick-cut bacon, Parmesan cheese, honey, red pepper, pumpkin purée, a dash of cinnamon, salt, pepper, and nutmeg. It never fails to impress! I sometimes adjust the recipe to accommodate my friends' unique dietary needs—omitting the bacon for vegetarians or substituting chicken for those who don't eat pork. But for this special occasion with my younger self, I'd make it just the way I like it, featuring some good ol' thick-cut country bacon.

Perhaps I'd also bake some never-failing Toll House cookies and set them in the oven. I'd light a candle and play a Steffany Gretzinger album in the background, creating the perfect atmosphere for what I consider to be real #church. I'd share with her the gospel of Jesus Christ and all the dreams He has for her life. I'd assure her that she's unique and special, and that God loves her just the way she is. There's no need to sacrifice anything, go anywhere, or adhere to religious dogmas to experience the living God.

I'd affirm that God cherishes her childlike wonder, her eagerness to be known by Him, and even her curiosity about the world around her. I'd let her know that self-care and rest are also God-given needs that He intends to meet. I'd invite her to share her passions, dreams, and concerns, and I'd lend a listening ear wherever she needs me to lean in. I'd ask her what led her to Christ, what struggles she's inviting Him into, and how I could support her journey.

Being authentic myself, I'd share my own Christian journey with her. I'd tell her where I got it right and where I faltered, and how I'm finding Jesus in the most unexpected places these days. Finally, I'd invite her to come again the next Sunday, just as she is, to continue doing church around the table, leaning into the beautiful gospel reality of loving and being loved—fully.

CAN I ASK YOU FOR A FAVOR CUTIE FRIEND?

IF YOU ENJOYED THIS BOOK AT ALL, WHICH I HOPE YOU DID! THEN PLEASE WRITE A REVIEW ON AMAZON OR YOUR PREFERRED PLATFORM TO BUY BOOKS! AS IT HELPS MORE THAN YOU KNOW! YOUR FEEDBACK MATTERS IN SPREADING THIS GOSPEL MESSAGE, SIS! THANK YOU FOR BEING A PART OF OUR READING COMMUNITY! I'VE ENJOYED THIS JOURNEY WITH YOU!

LET'S KEEP SPILLIN' THAT TEA! DISCOVER MORE RESOURCES AT MADDISENSPANO.COM.

TO STAY CONNECTED WITH MADDISEN OR TO BECOME A PART OF HER GROWING COMMUNITY OF JESUS-LOVERS, FOLLOW ALONG HERE:

INSTAGRAM: @MADDISENSPANO
TIKTOK: @MADDISENSPANO

ANDDDD I WOULD LOVE TO HEAR FROM YOU FRIEND!
IF YOU WANT TO CHAT, LIKE, ACTUALLY CHAT, ADD MY NUMBER TO YOUR CONTACTS: 813-382-3930. I'D LOVE TO HEAR FROM YOU BECAUSE IF YOU'VE MADE IT THIS FAR, I CONSIDER YOU LIKE A SISTER.

ABOUT THE AUTHOR

MADDISEN SPANO IS A—JESUS LOVER, COFFEE ENTHUSIAST, AND YOUR GO-TO GAL NEXT DOOR. WHETHER SHE'S DIVING DEEP INTO SCRIPTURE OR HAVING SOULFUL HEART-TO-HEARTS ON HER PORCH SWING WITH A STEAMING CUP OF HER FAVORITE BREW, HER LIFE IS AN OPEN BOOK—LITERALLY AND FIGURATIVELY! DURING HER DOWNTIME, MADDISEN LOVES CRAFTING ALONGSIDE HER LIVELY FIVE-YEAR-OLD AND SAVORING LIFE'S LITTLE JOYS WITH HER HUSBAND. SHE'S PENNED HER DEBUT BOOK, 'GOSPEL BEAUTIFULL,' AS A HEARTFELT LOVE LETTER TO WOMEN WHO'VE BEEN HURT, MISUNDERSTOOD, OR MARGI-NALIZED BY RELIGION. PASSIONATE ABOUT AUTHENTIC FAITH AND SPILLING THE GOSPEL TEA, SHE'S ON A MISSION TO GUIDE YOU OUT OF THE CHAOS AND INTO THE COMFORTING ARMS OF FREEDOM AND WHOLENESS IN CHRIST. SO GRAB YOUR FAVORITE MUG AND ALLOW HER TO JOURNEY TOGETHER WITH YOU TOWARD A FAITH THAT TRULY FILLS THE SOUL.

ENDNOTES

¹   McKeever, J. (2018, January 24). How Legalism Betrays Christ, Violates the Gospel, and Destroys People. Crosswalk.com. https://www.crosswalk.com/blogs/joe-mckeever/how-legalism-betrays-christ-violates-the-gospel-and-destroys-people.html

²   Carlisle, C. (2013, December 2). Is religion based on fear? The Guardian. https://www.theguardian.com/commentisfree/belief/2013/dec/02/bertrand-russell-philosopher-religion-fear-christian

³   Pascal, B. (1959). Pascal's Pensées: Selections (p. 114). Prabhat Prakashan.

⁴   Strong, J. (1990). Entry #7965, #7999. In Strong's Exhaustive Concordance of the Bible. T. Nelson.

⁵   Ricci, S. (2020, March 20). From stressed to shalom. Shalom Total Wellness. https://shalomtotalwellness.com/2020/03/20/from-stressed-to-shalom/

⁶   Gibson, L. C. (2015). Adult Children of Emotionally

Immature Parents. New Harbinger Publications.

7   Purvis, K., Qualls, L., & Pickett, E. (2020). The Connected
Parent. Harvest House Publishers

8   Jones, B. D. (2015, October 26). The dinner table as a
place of connection, brokenness, and blessing. Dallas Theological
Seminary. https://voice.dts.edu/article/a-place-at-the-table-jones-
barry/

9   Brown, B. (2010, June). The power of vulnerability [Video].
TED Talks. https://www.ted.com/talks/brene_brown_the_power_
of_vulnerability

10   Vaters, K. (2017, June 28). Jesus and crowds: The unhappy
marriage. Christianity Today. https://www.christianitytoday.com/
karl-vaters/2017/june/jesus-and-crowds-unhappy-marriage.html